BASIC RESEARCH STRATEGIES

A Guidebook for Stressed Thesis and Dissertation Writers

Dr. L.D. Molina, ScD, MPH

BASIC RESEARCH STRATEGIES
A GUIDEBOOK FOR STRESSED THESIS AND DISSERTATION WRITERS

iUniverse books may be ordered through booksellers or by contacting:

iUniverse
1663 Liberty Drive
Bloomington, IN 47403
www.iuniverse.com
1-800-Authors (1-800-288-4677)

ISBN: 978-1-4917-7479-3 (sc)
ISBN: 978-1-4917-7480-9 (e)

Print information available on the last page.

iUniverse rev. date: 08/24/2015

Images in this book are used with the permission of Richard Chapman, Lightbulb Cartoons, www.LightbulbCartoon.com and Randy Glasbergen Cartoon Service, www.glasbergen.com

For my students ... past, present, and future

"The greatest weapon against stress is our ability
to choose one thought over another."

– William James

Contents

Preface

Writing my doctoral dissertation was an overwhelming experience. In spite of completing several statistics courses, having to produce a data driven dissertation nearly paralyzed me. I convinced myself that I was fated to disappoint my family, friends, colleagues, faculty, and the National Institutes of Health who had generously supported me through four years of doctoral studies. My negative thought patterns were so severe that I developed a stress-induced acute respiratory condition. In her effort to help me put things into perspective, the Dean of Students explained that my condition was "stress induced", would pass, and that "a done thesis is a good thesis."

Although I remained determined not to ignore my potential, there was something about those simple words that were liberating. I shifted my attention toward keeping my expectations realistic and taking care of myself. The dissertation was completed, I graduated, and I eventually came to understand that the thesis was merely a "vehicle" for practicing critical skills useful for future work. Over the past decade, I have advised hundreds of students, who like me, deeply believe they are destined to change the world. And maybe they are. But the thesis period is not usually the time to test that assumption.

Finishing a graduate thesis is just one of the many challenges and complications life is likely to hand you. Most readers of this guidebook will be non-traditional students who carry the burden of balancing work, family, and multiple life pressures. Some research studies describe this interaction as a conflict on productivity, while other studies suggest the interaction is a facilitator on productivity. We therefore have the flexibility to shape perceptions of ourselves, our families, and workplace, as positive sources of empowerment during this journey.

Introduction

In many ways, the academic experience of today is considerably more challenging than only a decade ago. Currently, post-graduate students are typically forty years of age or older, have families for which to care, professions that demand high performance, and are charged with keeping everything in balance. They are what the education system term as "non-traditional" even though they represent the "new normal" and are the lifeblood of a rapidly burgeoning industry. The fastest growing segment of today's educational industry targets non-traditional students through online and blended learning formats. While these options significantly increase both flexibility and access for the student, they also have a downside.

Designed to respond to the demands of mid-career students, most accelerated online programs offer the promise of degree completion in half the time as traditional brick and mortar programs. The priority shifts to the expedient completion of a credential for career advancement, over a full exploratory learning experience. The pace of many accelerated programs can be appealing while also creating a different type of stress. The rapidity often denies the student opportunities to learn and practice basic skills needed to conduct successful independent research. To complicate matters further, it is important to recognize that over 75 percent of all college and university faculty and 90 percent of faculty at proprietary institutions consist of poorly compensated part-time adjunct professors. These faculty members typically hold multiple university appointments or are employment elsewhere for additional income.[1][2] Rarely available to

---

[1] Segran, E. The Adjunct Revolt: How Poor Professors Are Fighting Back, The Atlantic, April 28, 2014.

[2] Fruscione, J. When a college contracts 'adjunctivitis,' it's the students who lose, PBS News Hour, WGBH, July 25, 2014

provide the level of engagement the thesis writer needs, this structure can result in a high degree of frustration for both students and faculty.

Stress can be induced by the entire thesis process. However, a gap in understanding research basics is not usually evident until the thesis process begins. Many thesis writers can be quite comfortable with their subject matter, yet face difficulties with how to choose a methodology or approach for data analysis. This short guidebook was organized with the intention of providing basic information useful to students facing the demanding task of producing a graduate thesis.

The layout is as follows: Chapter 1: Talks about changes in the education industry over the past decade. It also speaks to the collective experience of stress and other emotional challenges experienced by students. Chapter 2: Provides an overview of elements to consider when pulling together a thesis proposal such as choosing a topic, asking questions, formulating hypotheses statements, and deciding what research designs to use. Chapter 3: Helps the reader determine a sample size and composition. Chapter 4: Introduces basic statistical concepts useful for analyzing data. Chapter 5: Provides ways to present and report data. Chapter 6: Talks about the final elements a thesis writer must consider. Chapter 7: Lists things to avoid during the thesis defense. The guidebook closes with a knowledge check, definition of terms, and some recommended resources.

Our bodies are hard-wired to react to stress in ways meant to protect you against threats from predators and other aggressors. But sometimes, we can be our own worst enemies by compounding existing stress. It's difficult to protect ourselves when we are unaware of this paradox. It is hoped that some of the material shared is useful for reminding the reader to make manageable choices as they navigate through what promises to be a challenging experience.

Chapter 1. Stress is Common!

Students may be particularly vulnerable to stress and depression. Graduate students struggling to complete a thesis requirement, commonly experience some level of depression, anxiety, or stress. Feeling a sense of emotional imbalance is a lot more common than you might think! In a recent study conducted by the University of California, Berkeley, 47% of doctoral students and 37% of master's degree students reportedly met the Diagnostic and Statistical Manual (DSM) criteria for depression.[3] Another study conducted by the University of Michigan estimated that over a quarter of their graduate students either took medication or received counseling for depression or anxiety.[4] Over half of PhD candidates at traditional mortar universities never graduate, and those who do finish, take an average of 9

---

[3]   Staff writers, (2015) U.C., Berkeley graduate students exhibit high rates of depression, survey says, The Daily Californian, University of California, Berkeley. Wednesday, April 22, 2015.

[4]   The Conversation (2015) Depression common on college campuses; graduate students more at risk http://www.psypost.org/2015/05/depression-common-on-college-campuses-graduate-students-more-at-risk-34158, May 9, 2015.

years to complete their degree.[5] Nearly half a decade is typically spent just writing the dissertation. This kind of time commitment comes at the cost of social development, family relationships, financial debt, stress, and one's ability to experience happiness and wellness.

Changes in Educational Models

The Institute of Education Sciences (IES) reports that the number of Americans graduating from college surged to 33.5 percent in 2013. This figure compares to 24.7 percent in 1995 and 21.9 percent in 1975. Over the past decade, completion of the Bachelor degree has increased by 137 percent while Master's and Doctoral degrees have increased by 254 percent and 170 percent respectively. Over 925,000 post-graduate credentials, which include 170,000 doctorates, were earned in 2013. [6] [7] [8] While IES degree completion figures do not distinguish between U.S. and foreign students, or brick and mortar and online degrees, it is safe to conclude that Higher Education is a rapidly growing industry in the United States.

Some attribute an increase in graduate degree completion to changes in industry standards. I would argue that the technological revolution has had a far more significant impact on the sharp and sudden increases in post-secondary education. The World Wide Web, invented by M.I.T. professor, Tim Berners-Lee, released the first publically available message on August 6, 1991. Pioneering web-based degree programs became available only four short years later. In 1995, because computer use was still in its infancy, there was little incentive for students to consider online or blended learning (combined web-based and face-to-face classroom instruction). In addition, most reputable businesses wanted nothing to do with degrees earned

---

[5]   http://www.phdcompletion.org/information/executive_summary_demographics _book_ii.pdf.

[6]   Lindley, J. & Machin, S. The boom in postgraduate education and its' impact on wage inequality. Center for Economic Performance, London School of Economics, Economics Report, November 20, 2013.

[7]   U.S. Department of Education, Institute of Education Sciences, National Center for Education Statistics, 20014.

[8]   https://nces.ed.gov/programs/digest/d13/tables/dt13_318.20.asp

through online education, as they were considered worth little more than products of paper mills.

Two decades later, perceptions regarding online learning are radically different. Use of computers and access to the Internet is now ubiquitous. In 2013, the U.S. census reported that 83.8 percent of U.S. households reported computer ownership, while 74.4 percent used the Internet.[9] The University of Phoenix and Kaplan University were among the first to receive regional accreditation. By 2015, the U.S. Department of Education reported that over 50 percent of all universities offer online graduate degrees, while approximately 65 percent of four-year post-secondary institutions and 97 percent of public two-year institutions provide credit-granting online learning.[10] This form of education delivery has increased five-fold in just one decade, far outpacing the growth of traditional brick and mortar institutions. On the negative side, degree completion rates have been reported to be as low as 20 percent, particularly among proprietary colleges with open admission policies.[11]

Recent changes within certain industries, such as healthcare, have had a remarkable impact on the online education model. The health care system is growing more dependent on doctorally trained allied health practitioners in audiology, pharmacology, occupational therapy, physical therapy, and nursing. An example of professional support of this transition can be found in The American Association of Colleges of Nursing (AACN) which voted to require Advanced Practice Nurses (APRN) earn a doctorate. This has resulted in the expansion of the Doctor of Nursing Practice (DNP), a terminal professional degree that includes advanced practice, diagnoses, treatment of diseases, and prepares registered nurses to become independent advanced practitioners. June 2015, the AACN reported that 264 Doctors of Nursing Practice (DNP) degree programs were operational

---

[9]   Unites States Census, 2013. Computer and Internet Use in the United States: 2013 By Thom File and Camille Ryan Issued November 2014 From: http://www.census.gov/history/pdf/2013computeruse.pdf

[10] U.S. Department of Education, Institute of Education Sciences, National Center for Education Statistics, 20014.

[11] Haynie, D. Experts Debate Graduation Rates for Online Students. Studies show online students may have lower completion rates than on-campus students, but the data are complex. U.S. News World Report, Jan. 30, 2015.

and an additional 60 DNP degree programs were in the planning stages across 48 states and the District of Columbia. In one academic year, enrollment of DNP students increased from 14,688 in 2013 to 18,352 in 2014, while the number of DNP graduates rose from 2,443 to 3,065 during the same period.[12] [13] Nearly all current DNP programs are offered as web-based or blended learning curricula.

Unlike non-clinical Ph.D.'s, clinical practice doctorates emphasize skills and knowledge needed to provide healthcare at a higher level. Clinical programs do however require the completion of a capstone or practice project to demonstrate writing, research, and statistical proficiencies. Unfortunately, many students in accelerated clinical practice programs do not have enough opportunity to learn the skills needed to complete a capstone or practice project.

Chronic Stress and Health

Thesis writing is a daily experience that spans over a long period of time. Therefore thesis induced stress would be assumed to be "chronic". Chronic stress is different from the more common "acute" form of stress, which is short-term, occasional, and more easily recognized. Already under pressure to meet the demands of adult life, chronic stress experienced by non-traditional students can be exasperating. Yet, university administrators, faculty, and students do not openly speak about this phenomenon.

Animal and human studies have linked physical and psychological stress with organ systems, respiratory distress, and serious problems related to the immune system.[14] The National Institutes of Health list the following conditions as resulting from chronic stress:

---

[12] American Association for Colleges of Nursing (AACN), DNP Fact Sheet, June 6, 2015

[13] J.B., Ivey, Health Policy and the DNP Student. Topics in Advanced Practice Nursing eJournal. 2008; 8 (4).

[14] A. Palok, Potter, A. Griebel, P. Modern approaches to understanding stress and disease susceptibility: A review with special emphasis on respiratory disease, International Journal of General Medicine 2009:2 19–32.

- Anxiety and Panic attacks
- Back and Neck pain
- Cardiovascular problems
- Chronic fatigue syndrome
- Depression
- High blood pressure
- Increase in blood sugar levels
- Irritable bowel problems
- Rapid heartbeat, heart palpitations
- Respiratory problems, heavy breathing
- Skin conditions (eczema)
- Sleep problems (insomnia, oversleeping)
- Stomach problems (acid reflux, ulcers)
- Tension headaches or migraines
- Upset stomach (ulcers and acid reflux)
- Weakened immune system

Graduate students as a group are a classic example of "over-achievers" who set unrealistically high goals and do not allow much room for flexibility or adjustment. Many students can compound the stress experience by failing to realize that the knowledge and ability is not fixed, but in fact, is elastic and can change.[15] Another common misconception is that the thesis or dissertation must be "perfect". Stay open to the experience of the intellectual growth and development that is likely to occur. It is common to feel inadequate when beginning the thesis process. But, your sense of self-efficacy will grow substantially as you move along the process.

When one considers the time commitment and stress involved with completing a graduate degree, it is easy to understand why so many individuals elect to take an easier, and sometimes, illegal way out. In 2013, over 3,400 diploma mills were identified as responsible for the annual sale of approximately 50,000 counterfeit doctorates in administration,

---

[15] Dweck, C., (2007) Mindset: The New Psychology of Success, Random House Publishing.

computer science, education, law, medicine, psychology, and other fields.[16] Many sources have been known to sell original dissertations and theses for a hefty fee. Sadly, countless high level government and academic officials falsely claim to have earned a doctoral degree. Among them are the former Dean of Admissions of the Massachusetts Institute of Technology[17] and the former Director of Homeland Security.[18]

I share this information to point out that "earning" a doctorate requires a considerable amount of work, focus, and determination that not everyone is prepared to invest. I have worked with dozens of students who have threatened to drop out of their program. Some have even thought about "purchasing" a written dissertation because they had no more fuel left to continue. When we are tired and fatigued the quality of our decisions fade. Later reflection may result in regretting poor choices. One can wage that most individuals who elect to drop out, or worse, purchase a fake credential, allow stress to impair their decision-making.

For purposes of this guidebook, stress scores were measured among a sample of thesis writers using the DASS-21. This scale asks 21 questions or 7 questions for three subscales including (1) depression, (2) anxiety, and (3) stress. Subscale scores range between 0 and 21 points. The overall DASS has strong reliability with a Cronbach's alpha for American, British, and Australian adults estimated at .94 and subtest values estimated between 0.72 and 0.76 for medical students. The principal value of the DASS is to clarify the locus of emotional disturbance of core symptoms of depression, anxiety and stress but does not offer diagnoses according to classification systems such as the Diagnostic and Statistical Manual (DSM) and the International Classification of Diseases (ICD).[19]

---

[16] AlterNet / *By John Bear, Allen Ezell*, Does Your Doctor Have a Fake One can? The Billion-Dollar Industry That Has Sold Over a Million Fake Diplomas. retrieved June 18, 2013 from: http://www.alternet.org/story/155864

[17] Z. M. Seward, MIT Admissions Dean Resigns after Fake Degrees Come to Light, Diplomas from three schools were fabricated, school officials say, *The Crimson,* Harvard University, April 26, 2007.

[18] R. Leung, Diplomas for Sale, Reports On Online Diploma Mills, CBS News. Nov. 8, 2004

[19] Agency for Clinical Innovation, Australia (2015). From: http://www.aci.health.nsw. gov.au/__data/assets/pdf_file/0019/212905/DASS_21_with_scoring_BB.pdf

© Randy Glasbergen / glasbergen.com

I + I = II

"If you want a better answer, ask a better question!"

Chapter 2. Elements of a Research Proposal

Choosing a Topic

Choosing a topic is the first of many steps in designing your thesis or dissertation. Topic selection is not a simple task and is perhaps the most challenging aspect of getting started. Most graduate students nowadays currently qualify as mid-career professionals who have some level of knowledge or expertise in a particular field. Perhaps you can make use of that understanding for purposes of conducting a study. I commonly work with students who never considered a topic relevant to their professional work. For students who are mid-career professionals, choosing a topic that can be conducted and applied to the current workplace, increases viability and chances that the thesis will be completed. A thesis can be an opportunity to collect new information useful for enhancing the operational priorities of the organization or business that employs you.

I once coached a thesis writer who was a mid-level program director at a social service agency. She wanted to study the relationship between leadership style and work motivation. With no specific interest in the publishing industry, she had planned to study a group of editors, simply because she knew someone in the industry. She also assumed they would be easy to access without fully understanding what was involved with getting IRB permission to study a sample. I asked why she had not considered her own workplace as a viable option. After thinking about the resources she could potentially tap at her place of employment, she decided to change the focus of her study. She presented the purpose of the study to the executive management team and was granted permission to conduct the study with the staff of her organization. The study outcomes were compelling enough to be used for developing new strategies for enhancing staff motivation and positive organizational behavior. Her findings were so helpful with creating positive change, that she was promoted to an executive level position within a year!

I do not wish to imply that all work situations work out so seamlessly. But it's important to consider the practical options when choosing a research topic. Remember that choosing a topic is like choosing a partner or spouse. For better or for worse, your thesis will become your closest companion for a year or two, or longer. According to the Centers for Disease Control, around 50 percent of marriages in the United States will end in divorce. Meanwhile, the Council of Graduate Schools Ph.D. Completion Project reports that about 50 percent of doctorate students will never complete their dissertation! The parallel is clear.

When choosing a topic, consider:

1. Research or practical work you've already done.
2. Your own interests.
3. Current events or timely issues.

EXAMPLE: My work with graduate students has led me to believe that stress is more pronounced during the thesis period. Stress experienced among graduate students has been examined, but stress among those engaged in the graduate thesis process is less understood. Understanding this phenomenon is important for preserving student integrity and program completion rates.

Minimize Variables, Avoid Clutter

As you read more and learn more about your topic over time, you will be tempted to grow your thesis. Try to exercise boundaries and apply limits. Problems often occur when you have too many potential ideas from which to choose. An excess of ideas from different sources can create *clutter,* disorganized thinking, and becomes draining to manage. Clutter creates feelings of "suffocation" or the inability to breathe". Too many variables can bog you down, cause confusion, and lead to anxiety and depression. Do not "over-consume" and keep variables to a minimum. Limit yourself to a few variables to prevent the risk of inheriting a topic too complex and may no longer be doable.

Original data collection is sensitive to time required of participants. Longer studies collecting more variables and can a potentially lower the number of individuals willing to participate in your study. Common response rates vary by discipline and study method, typically ranging between 50-80 percent. It is always the goal to get as many individuals you invite to participate. Choose a topic you can comfortably complete, rather than one that may seem more impressive but never gets finished. Thoughtful selection of few variables is more impactful in the long run.

EXAMPLE: Data for 4 variables included age, gender, degree, and score for a 7 item DASS stress test. DASS scores were used to create categories of severity (normal, mild, moderate, severe, and very severe) as suggested by the scale's authors.[20] A case report is provided below.

---

[20] Agency for Clinical Innovation, Australia (2015). From: http://www.aci.health.nsw. gov.au/__data/assets/pdf_file/0019/212905/DASS_21_with_scoring_BB.pdf

Dr. L.D. Molina, ScD, MPH

Case Summaries[a]

	Gender	Degree	Age Group	DASS (pre) Stress Score	DASS Stress Level (pre)	DASS (post) Stress Score	DASS Stress Level (post)
1	Female	Doctorate	Over 50	8	Mild	8	Mild
2	Female	Doctorate	40-49	18	Extremely Severe	16	Severe
3	Male	Masters	Over 50	21	Extremely Severe	18	Extremely Severe
4	Female	Masters	40-49	14	Severe	13	Severe
5	Male	Masters	40-49	14	Severe	14	Severe
6	Female	Masters	40-49	21	Extremely Severe	18	Extremely Severe
7	Female	Doctorate	30-39	15	Severe	14	Severe
8	Male	Masters	40-49	8	Mild	8	Mild
9	Female	Doctorate	40-49	18	Extremely Severe	18	Extremely Severe
10	Female	Doctorate	40-49	15	Severe	12	Moderate
11	Female	Doctorate	Over 50	21	Extremely Severe	18	Extremely Severe
12	Female	Masters	40-49	12	Moderate	11	Moderate
13	Female	Doctorate	30-39	16	Severe	14	Severe
14	Female	Doctorate	Over 50	14	Severe	12	Moderate
15	Female	Masters	30-39	14	Severe	12	Moderate
16	Female	Doctorate	Over 50	18	Extremely Severe	16	Severe
17	Female	Doctorate	40-49	16	Severe	15	Severe
18	Female	Masters	30-39	9	Mild	8	Mild
19	Female	Doctorate	30-39	11	Moderate	11	Moderate
20	Female	Doctorate	30-39	7	Normal	6	Normal
21	Female	Doctorate	Over 50	8	Mild	8	Mild
22	Female	Masters	Over 50	9	Mild	6	Normal
23	Female	Doctorate	40-49	8	Mild	6	Normal
24	Female	Masters	30-39	11	Moderate	10	Moderate
25	Male	Masters	Over 50	20	Extremely Severe	18	Extremely Severe
26	Female	Masters	40-49	14	Severe	13	Severe
27	Male	Masters	40-49	15	Severe	12	Moderate
28	Female	Masters	40-49	21	Extremely Severe	20	Extremely Severe
29	Female	Doctorate	30-39	15	Severe	14	Severe
30	Male	Masters	40-49	10	Moderate	10	Moderate
31	Female	Doctorate	Over 50	8	Mild	7	Normal
32	Female	Doctorate	40-49	18	Extremely Severe	16	Severe
33	Male	Masters	Over 50	21	Extremely Severe	19	Extremely Severe
34	Female	Masters	40-49	14	Severe	12	Moderate
35	Male	Masters	40-49	14	Severe	12	Moderate
36	Female	Masters	40-49	21	Extremely Severe	16	Severe
37	Female	Doctorate	30-39	15	Severe	13	Severe
38	Male	Masters	40-49	8	Mild	6	Normal
39	Female	Doctorate	40-49	18	Extremely Severe	12	Moderate
40	Female	Doctorate	40-49	15	Severe	12	Moderate
41	Female	Doctorate	Over 50	21	Extremely Severe	19	Extremely Severe
42	Female	Masters	40-49	12	Moderate	11	Moderate
43	Female	Doctorate	30-39	16	Severe	15	Severe
44	Female	Doctorate	Over 50	14	Severe	14	Severe
45	Female	Masters	30-39	14	Severe	13	Severe
46	Female	Doctorate	Over 50	18	Extremely Severe	15	Severe
47	Female	Doctorate	40-49	16	Severe	16	Severe
48	Female	Masters	30-39	9	Mild	7	Normal
49	Female	Doctorate	30-39	11	Moderate	12	Moderate
50	Female	Doctorate	30-39	7	Normal	6	Normal
51	Female	Doctorate	Over 50	8	Mild	8	Mild
52	Female	Masters	Over 50	9	Mild	8	Mild
53	Female	Doctorate	40-49	8	Mild	8	Mild
54	Female	Masters	30-39	11	Moderate	10	Moderate
55	Male	Masters	Over 50	20	Extremely Severe	20	Extremely Severe
56	Female	Masters	40-49	14	Severe	13	Severe
57	Male	Masters	40-49	15	Severe	12	Moderate
58	Female	Masters	40-49	21	Extremely Severe	18	Extremely Severe
59	Female	Doctorate	30-39	15	Severe	13	Severe
60	Male	Masters	40-49	10	Moderate	9	Mild
Total	N	60	60	60	60	60	60

a. Limited to first 100 cases

10

Relevant Questions

After a topic has been identified, you should develop question(s) that help you probe your topic. A thesis is a scholarly argument surrounding a clear question. A good thesis question may come from curious observations or an observed need. Do not be afraid to ask a question that challenges conventional wisdom or tests what seems to be a clear-cut topic. There are many questions you might want to ask for your general topic. Try to consider questions that you find interesting, relevant, and met with the least constraint. Treat the question(s) as an opportunity to look at a topic from a unique and thoughtful way. Once your questions are clarified, you are on your way to a solid thesis study.

A research question can set boundaries to help you figure out where to go next. A research question defines which data you need to collect and which methods you will need to use to access and analyze your documents. Because research is rarely a linear process, as you collect data, your question is likely to change and grow. Remember to limit the number of questions you are going to research. One could ask many questions regarding stress experienced by thesis writers. For purposes of this project, I am limiting myself to five questions.

EXAMPLE:

1. Do thesis writers experience more stress than the general student population?
2. Are levels of stress among thesis writers different between masters' and doctoral candidates?
3. Are stress levels among thesis writers different between gender groups?
4. Are stress levels among thesis writers different between age groups?
5. Do stress levels decline after the thesis is completed?

Hypotheses Statements

Research questions and hypotheses are often used interchangeably, but they are very different. A research question serves as the initial step in a research project and can be asked once you have an idea of what you want to study. By comparison, a hypothesis is a proposed explanation for a phenomenon. The term derives from the Greek, *hypotithenai* meaning "to put under" or "to suppose". A hypothesis is confirmed by observation or an experiment. Scientific theories are developed from using a hypothesis as a method to gather evidence and test its' accuracy.

Quantitative studies usually require consideration of a hypothesis. Your "hypothesis statements" are the foci of your thesis. They should reflect specific predictions of what you expect will happen in your study. While a single quantitative study may have several hypotheses, it is recommended that you propose testing as few hypotheses as possible. By contrast, a qualitative or exploratory study does not have a formal hypothesis, but rather, may explore a question which will be further explored in a future study.

Whenever you write a hypothesis, you are creating *two* hypotheses or formulating two opposite hypothesis statements. One statement describes your prediction and one describes all the other possible outcomes. Predictions can be described as the Null (Ho) and Alternative (Ha) hypotheses. Your prediction (Ha) is that variable A and variable B will be correlated or related somehow. The other possible outcome (Ho) would be that variable A and variable B are *not* correlated or related.

Usually, we call the hypothesis that supports your prediction the **alternative** hypothesis and hypothesis that describes NO relationship the **null** hypothesis. It can be helpful to remember that the Latin translation for **"nothing"** is **"null"**, therefore the **null hypothesis = no difference**. If your prediction specifies a direction, we call this a **one-tailed hypothesis**. A hypothesis that does not specify a direction would be a **two-tailed hypothesis**. Remember that your prediction (directional or not) as the **alternative** or second hypothesis, and the first is the **null hypothesis.**

When your data collection and data analysis are completed, you will have to choose between the two hypotheses. If your prediction was correct, then you (usually) reject the null hypothesis and accept the alternative. If your alternative prediction (difference) was not supported by the data, then you will accept the null hypothesis (no difference) and reject the alternative. This logic may seem an awkward way to test a research hypothesis. It encompasses a long tradition in statistics called the *hypothetico-deductive method* used to prevent falsification of a test on observable data.

EXAMPLE:

First hypothesis:
H_0: There is no difference in the level of stress experienced by thesis writers and the general student population.
H_a: There is a difference in the level of stress experienced by thesis writers and the general student population.

Second hypothesis:
H_0: Stress levels are not different between masters' and doctoral students.
H_a: Stress levels are different between masters' and doctoral students.

Third hypothesis:
H_0: Stress levels are not different between gender groups.
H_a: Stress levels are different between gender groups.

Fourth hypothesis:
H_0: Stress levels are no different between age groups.
H_a: Stress levels are different between age groups.

Fifth hypothesis:
H_0: There is no difference in stress levels before and after the completion of the thesis.
H_a: There is a difference in stress levels before and after completion of the thesis.

Research Methodologies

The study design is the process used to answer your research questions, prove or disprove your hypothesis, and if a randomized scientific study, test cause-and-effect relationships between your study variables. You should choose a design strategy based access to resources as well as its usefulness for achieving your intended research goals.[21] Your research question will dictate the kind of research methodology to use. If you wish to collect quantitative data, you are likely measuring variables to verify or question an existing theory or hypothesis. Some individuals prefer to verify questions and hypothesis through the use of numbers and statistics. Others do not think statistics and number provide enough meaning to answer questions and rather use qualitative forms of data. The choice relies on your preference and what you want to study.

Quantitative

Quantitative research design is the standard method of most scientific disciplines. This type of design is seen as a more true science and uses traditional mathematical and statistical means to measure results and draw conclusions. While physical and clinical scientists most commonly use quantitative studies, this method is also widely used in the behavioral and social sciences, education, and economics. Quantitative data can be gathered through the use of survey data, questionnaires, scales, records, pre-existing, or secondary data sets.

These types of studies use a standard format for generating a hypothesis that is to be proved or disproved. Hypotheses must be provable by statistical means and is the basis by which an experiment is designed. Randomization of study groups is considered essential whenever possible. A sound quantitative design should manipulate only one variable at a time, or an analysis can become burdensome. Ideally, the research should be designed in a manner that allows others to repeat the experiment.

---

[21] McLeod, S. A. (2007). *Experimental Design - Simply Psychology.* Retrieved from http://www.simplypsychology.org/experimental-designs.html

Non-Experimental Designs

Non-experimental research studies do not require the researcher to control, manipulate or alter the predictor variable or subjects. Typically, this means the non-experimental researcher must rely on correlations, surveys, or case studies. Findings cannot demonstrate a true cause-and-effect relationship. Three common non-experimental research designs include:

Cross-Sectional Design: One or more groups of subjects are studied at one given point in time.

Medical Record Review (MRR): Prerecorded, patient-focused data as the primary source of information to answer a research question. Sources of information include physician and nursing notes, ambulance call reports, diagnostic tests, clinic, administrative, and government records or computerized databases.[22]

Surveys: Questionnaires conducted in person, by phone, or online.

Experimental Designs

Experimental Designs reflect studies where a researcher is able to manipulate the predictor variable and subjects to identify a cause-and-effect relationship. Experimental studies typically require that one group is placed in an experimental group (manipulated) while the other is placed in a placebo group (non-manipulated). This type of design is considered the "gold standard" against which all other designs are judged. A well-designed experimental design is probably the strongest design with respect to internal validity, which is at the center of all causal inferences.[23] Experimental Designs also control factors such as randomization and manipulation of the independent variable.

---

[22] Worster A. and Ted Haines, T, Advanced Statistics: Understanding Medical Record Review (MRR) Studies, Academy of Emergency Medicine, February 2004, Vol. 11, No. 2.

[23] W. Trochim, (2006) Research Methods Knowledge Base. Retrieved From: http://www.socialresearchmethods.net/kb/desexper.php

If you decide an experiment is the best approach to testing your hypothesis, then you need to design the experiment. The most common way to design an experiment in the social and behavioral sciences is to divide the participants into two groups - the experimental group and the control group. The change is introduced for the experimental group and not the control group. In terms of a pre and post study design, changes in the post group are measured in the context of their exposure to an agent, intervention, or training. The researcher must decide how they will allocate their sample such as sample size, and assigned participation in one or both conditions. The three Types of Experimental Designs most commonly referenced are:

Case Control: The classic experimental design specifies an experimental group and a control group. The experimental or case group is exposed to something, but the control group is not exposed. Subsequent experimental designs include comparing the experiences of the same respondents before and after exposure to something (independent variable).

Cohort (Longitudinal): One or more groups of subjects are examined simultaneously with the intention of inferring trends over a period of time. The assumption is that the phenomenon under study changes with time. Time data examines sequence and patterns of change, growth, or trends across time; into the future (prospective) and back from the past (retrospective). Trend data are collected at predetermined time intervals from samples selected from the general population.

Pre-Post Tests: Pre and post testing is a widely used method for assessing how an intervention has had an impact on study participants. The process should entail a (pre) test to determine the starting level. At a later point, an exactly comparable (post) test is administered to determine the extent to which a change has occurred and to determine if changes between the two testing periods are significant.

It is important to realize that rarely can changes be attributable to the intervention alone. Other factors (co-variables) and timing of an intervention can have a critical impact on the results. In addition, post-testing results vary considerably depending on how soon the test is administered after the respondent has been exposed to the intervention. A two-sample t-test is typically used to measure pre and post (intervention) differences.

Quasi-Experimental Design

A quasi-experiment is similar to an experimental design. The main difference is that quasi-experimental designs lack randomly assigned groups. When performing an experiment, the researcher is attempting to demonstrate if one variable influence another variable. Cause and effect can be achieved only if assignments are random. Quasi-experimental designs follow the same design formats as experimental designs. However, because the assignments are not random, inferences made to the population, which the sample is meant to represent, must be approached with caution.

Qualitative

Qualitative methods are probably the oldest of all scientific techniques, with Ancient Greek philosophers qualitatively observing the world around them and trying to come up with answers which explained what they saw. Natural philosophy from Latin *philosophia naturalis* was the philosophical study of nature and the physical universe, and the dominant before the development of modern science.[24]

Qualitative studies are based on open-ended queries questions and use in-depth probing to uncover the thoughts and feelings behind initial responses. This type of design requires a degree of creativity and subjectivity that quantitative studies do not. Qualitative approaches come from a variety of schools of thought including grounded theory, ethnography, and community participatory research and have grown out of disciplines like cultural, anthropology, psychology, and sociology. Data can be gathered from a number of approaches including interviews, focus groups, observation, stories, field notes, journals, archives, diaries, photography,

---

[24]   Crowe, M. J. (2007) *Mechanics from Aristotle to Einstein,* Santa Fe, NM: Green Lion Press.

and videos. These methods permit a more in-depth and descriptive understanding of a phenomenon than quantitative research usually allows.

Qualitative research is sometimes used as a precursor to quantitative research. It can be used to generate ideas that can be used to formulate testable hypotheses using a quantitative approach. Qualitative methods are flexible, do not follow any one standard structure, and therefore require careful construction in design. Qualitative research methods continually evolve as styles of human interaction and communication change. Given the objectives of a particular study, the researcher should decide and provide the most appropriate interview setting. Commonly used qualitative methods include:

Focus group: A focus group involves use of a moderator to lead a group discussion. Participants share thoughts, experiences and opinions relevant to the research question(s). Focus groups are typically one to two hours in length and can vary in size, although an optimal size is between four and eight participants. They can be held in person (face-to-face) or remotely by teleconferencing, video conferencing, text chat, online bulletin boards, or other forms of web-based conferencing.

In-depth interview (IDI): Interview with a single individual, typically lasting between 30 to 90 minutes, depending on the subject matter and context. IDIs may be conducted in a number of environments such as the respondent's home or workplace, research facility, public location, or telephone.

Dyads, Triads: In-depth interviews with two or three people who represent members of the same family, team, or group, and collectively make decisions relevant to the research.

Paired interviews: Consecutive interviews conducted with two people who share a product, service, or other experience together. Examples include married couples, parent and child, and other dual partnerships.

Qualitative techniques are extremely useful when a subject is complex and cannot provide simple yes/no or categorical responses to answer questions.

Many students prefer to conduct qualitative studies because this method is widely believed to be easier to plan and carry out than quantitative studies. Although qualitative studies do not require the use of math or statistics, they can be much more difficult to perform correctly. Students are often not properly trained to collect and analyze qualitative data, which can result in an inability to generate meaningful data, rejection by a thesis or peer-review committee, and wasted time.

Mixed Method

The term, "mixed method" refers to the manner in which a researcher integrates both qualitative and quantitative data within a single study. The mixed method approach to conducting empirical research can have many advantages for gaining insights on interesting phenomena and expands the research in a way a single approach cannot. The process of conducting statistical analysis complemented by observation, offers a broader landscape of information from which to develop more hypotheses, advance discussions, and contemplate future research.

Table. 2.1. Research question/Hypothesis and possible Method and Statistical Test(s)

Question/Hypothesis	Method	Statistical Test
Is there a relationship between Genders, Age (continuous), and Stress Scores (continuous)?	Quantitative	(Pearson's) Correlation
Is there a relationship between Gender and Stress CATEGORIES?	Quantitative	Chi-Square
Is there a significant difference in average DASS Stress Scores between two degree levels (Masters v Doctorate)?	Quantitative	T-Test
Is the relationship between stress CATEGORIES and age group significant?	Quantitative	Chi-Square
Are there significant differences in average DASS Stress Scores between three or more age groups?	Quantitative	Analysis of Variance (ANOVA)
Do average DASS Stress scores change before and after completion of the thesis?	Quantitative	Two samples (Paired) T-test.
Do thesis writers experience a higher stress level than the university student population?	Quantitative	One sample T-Test
How has thesis related stress has affected your relationships with your spouse/family?	Qualitative	Interview (dyad, triad), focus group
Describe how the thesis process has affected your sense of wellbeing.	Qualitative	In depth one on one interview (IDI).
What types of support do you feel would be helpful to graduate thesis writers?	Mixed Methods	Survey, open ended questions, interview, focus group.

Chapter 3. Deciding WHO to study

Sample Selection

Sample selection is a critically important but sometimes underestimated part of a research study. Much time can be saved by selecting a sample of individuals from a population to whom you have easy access such as co-workers, colleagues, or members of an organization to which you belong. Seldom is the population of the people in which you are interested, small enough to test everyone. When it is not possible to survey everybody, you will need to select a sample. Results based on the sample of in your study, give you an estimate of what might have occurred among the whole population had they been surveyed. The sampling approach you choose depend upon the purpose of the study and resources (time/money) you have to commit to sample selection.

Random Sample Selection

The first question you need to ask yourself is whether a random or non-random sample is appropriate for your study. In general, when collecting quantitative data, random sampling is considered the "golden standard". Random samples are also known as 'probability' samples because every member of the population of interest will have an equal chance (equal probability) of being selected to participate in the study. The purpose of random selection is to avoid bias in selection and to assure that your sample reflects the true diversity of your study population. While this method typically requires more resources, it increases the ability of the researcher to make inferences to the population from which the sample was drawn.

Before you decide to select a random sample, you need to specify the characteristics of the people you want to include. For example, do you only want to gather the views of females or people within a certain age range? The characteristics of your sample should reflect the characteristics of the population targeted by the intervention. For example, if you are evaluating an intervention aimed at changing the attitudes of female graduate students over 30, then your sample should consist of females over 30 years of age. If you want to compare this particular group to other demographic groups, you may also want to include males or students less than 30 years of age in your sample selection.

Research Randomizer

The Research Randomizer (www.Randomizer.org) is a free tool that can be extremely valuable to quickly generate random numbers or assign participants to experimental conditions. The service developed by Urbaniak and S. Plous, Executive Director of The Social Psychology Network for use by students, researchers and others interested in generating sets of random numbers. By 2015, this site has generated over 914 million sets of random numbers for a variety of purposes including psychology experiments, medical trials and survey research. The Research Randomizer has also received special recognition from professional organizations including the American Psychological Association (APA) and the University of Wisconsin Science and Engineering Scout Project. www.Randomizer.

org only requires a standard web browser (e.g., Chrome, Safari, Firefox, Internet Explorer) and no other software is needed.[25]

Non-Random Sampling

Non-Random or non-probability sampling represents a number of techniques for selecting a sample or units from a population the researcher is interested in studying. Unlike probability sampling, non-probability or non-random sampling techniques select samples based on the researchers' subjective judgment. Non-probability sampling can be used in quantitative, qualitative, and mixed method research designs. A quantitative research design using a non-randomized sampling is often viewed as an inferior alternative to randomized probability sampling techniques. The goal of random or probability sampling is to achieve objectivity in the selection of samples and to allow statistical inferences to be generalized to your population of interest.

While non-probability sampling techniques are often thought to be scientifically inferior to probability sampling techniques, there are strong practical reasons for using this type of sampling method particularly for qualitative research designs and exploratory research where the goal of the study is to explore an issue in a quick and inexpensive way. Non-random sampling techniques are generally easier, more cost effective, and less time consuming when compared with probability sampling. Your research question and strategy will influence the type of non-probability sampling method to use. Five types of non-probability sampling techniques most frequently used include (1) quota sampling, (2) convenience sampling, (3) purposive sampling, (4) self-selection sampling, and (5) snowball sampling.

Quota sampling

Quota sampling is used to acquire a sample where the strata or groups (e.g., male v. female students) are proportional to the population being studied. If differences between male and female students were to be examined, you

---

25   Urbaniak, G., & Plous, S. (2013). Research Randomizer (Version 4.0). Retrieved on [DATE] from http://www.randomizer.org.

would want to choose the gender of your participants based on the gender distribution of the student population.

Convenience sampling

Convenience sampling selects any respondents for inclusion in the sample who are the easiest to access. For example, among a total of 10,000 university students, if only interested in achieving a sample size of 100 students, the researcher might invite any students who might be willing to take part in the research.

Purposive sampling

Purposive sampling, also known as judgmental, selective or subjective sampling, requires the judgment of the researcher for selecting study participants. Purposive sampling techniques have a focus on certain types of respondents and might require a number of criteria for participation. An example of a purposeful sample needed could be (1) female (2) nursing students (3) studying in the state of California.

Self-Selection sampling

Self-selection sampling is appropriate when we want to allow individuals or organizations voluntarily. The key component is that research subjects volunteer to take part in the research rather than being approached by the researcher directly. Generating a self-selection sample involves (1) publicizing your need for participants, (2) checking that the potential participant meets basic criteria of the population you want to study, and (3) so either invite or reject their participation.

This method is useful when we want to allow individuals or organizations to freely decide to take part in research. Self-selection can be used with a wide range of research designs and research methods. An example is a survey posted online, inviting anyone within a particular organization or meeting a certain description to take part. Individuals may choose to participle because they have a personal interest in the topic or want to contribute to the outcomes.

Surveys can be created and posted through a number of online survey software services. One of the most popular services is Survey Monkey® which provides free and low cost, customizable surveys, data analysis, sample selection, bias elimination, and data representation tools. While they offer many services free of charge, the company now offers a host of more sophisticated services for a fee. One such service provides the selection of respondents from an audience of millions, to complete a survey. Respondents answering an online survey can be considered "self-selected".

Snowball sampling

Snowball sampling is particularly appropriate when interested in studying a hard-to-reach or hidden population that exhibits some kind of social stigma, behaviors, or other traits that make them socially marginalized. Snowball sampling is a non-probability based sampling technique that can be used to gain access to such populations who cannot be easily identified, for example, substance abusers, homeless, sex workers, and so forth. In some instances, there may be no other way of accessing your sample and snowball sampling may be the only viable sampling strategy for gathering respondents who are hard to reach.

A snowball sample typically requires two steps. (1) Identify one individual in the desired population; and (2) use this individual to find additional participants. Finding a number of individuals willing to identify themselves and take part in the research may be quite difficult, so the aim is to start with just one or two participants to start. The researcher should ask the initial participants who agreed to take part in the research, if they know of others who may be willing to take part. For ethical reasons, participants should come forward themselves rather than being identified by the researcher. The sampling should continue only until a sufficient sample size has been met. Because this sampling method is flexible and not systematic, snowball samples should not be considered to be representative of the population being studied.

EXAMPLE: Non-random techniques were used to select a sample of students who had sought thesis assistance between 2013 and 2014. The survey was created through Survey Monkey®, posted online and sent out to a group of 150 students and invited to complete the survey. All respondents self-selected and may have chosen to participate because they had a specific interest in the study, or wanted to reciprocate support to the researcher. The study was closed once the number of students needed to conduct the study was acquired.

Sample Size Estimate

Researchers will inevitably have to decide how many responses to include in their study. Many references suggest that N=30 is the magical number for acquiring a sample with a normal distribution. This number is arbitrary. In some situations, a smaller sample could be adequate. In other circumstances, a larger sample sizes may be required to provide enough "power" for assuring accurate results, making inferences, and avoiding Type I and Type II errors. Before calculating a sample size, you should determine a few parameters:

1. Population Size: How many people fit your demographic or the actual population you want to study? For instance, if you want to know about graduate students currently enrolled in a particular university, you would have to find out how many students are currently registered. If you cannot get an exact number, use as close an approximation as possible.
2. Confidence Level: The confidence level (CL) reflects how confident the actual mean falls within the confidence interval. The CL is commonly set at 90%, 95%, or 99%. The higher the CL, the larger the sample size will be estimated.
3. Confidence Interval (CI) or Margin of Error: Because no sample provides perfectly accurate responses, you need to decide how much error you will allow in your study. An example is a political poll that reports "70% of voters support a Proposition with a margin of error of +/- 5%". This suggests that between 65% and 75% actually support the proposition. Note that the higher the margin of error, the smaller your estimated sample size will be.

4. Because the study has not yet been conducted, the default percentage of 50% will automatically be used by the calculator to ensure that your sample will be large enough.

There are several free online calculators available to estimate a sample size. For this example, I used *Creative Research Systems* for its accuracy and ease of use. Once you have your values defined you can calculate the sample size needed for your study. Enter your choice of parameters in a calculator to find the sample size.

EXAMPLE: I have worked with about 150 students over the past two academic years. The total population size is therefore placed at 150. A (standard) 95% Confidence Level and a 10% Confidence Interval (Margin of Error) are the parameters chosen. Based on these parameters, a sample size of N=59 is estimated.[26]

Sample Size Calculator	
Confidence Level:	● 95% ○ 99%
Confidence Interval:	10
Population:	150
Sample size needed:	59

IRB Review

All study proposals go through an IRB review. Depending on who or what you decide to study will dictate how extensive a review your proposal will get through. An institutional review board (IRB) is formally designated to approve and monitor research involving humans. The IRB will conduct a risk-benefit analysis to determine whether or not research should be done.

---

[26] Source: http://www.surveysystem.com/sscalc.htm

The IRB review process is conducted to assure that appropriate steps are taken to protect the rights and welfare of study participants and to protect human subjects from physical or psychological harm. IRB's are commonly used for studies in the health, social, and behavioral sciences.

IRB's were initially developed in direct response to research abuses in the 20th century such as experiments performed by Nazi physicians during World War II, and the Tuskegee Syphilis Study, conducted between 1932 and 1972 by the U.S. Public Health Service. The result of many abuses both in the United States and Internationally was the National Research Act of 1974 and the development of the Belmont Report, which outlines the primary ethical principles in human subjects review including "respect for persons", "beneficence", and "justice."

An IRB may only approve research for which there is a *bona fide* informed consent process and for which the risks to subjects are balanced by potential benefits to society. In the United States, IRBs are governed by Title 45 Code of Federal Regulations Part 46. Students can complete an online Human Subjects training free of charge by the National Institutes of Health, Office of Extramural Research entitled "Protecting Human Research Participants". Visit https://phrp.nihtraining.com to register and complete the free online training. Note that although NIH offers a comprehensive introduction to this topic, most universities have preferred methods and resources for training degree candidates in research ethics.

All degree candidates performing research involving human subjects are required to go through an IRB review. The IRB review process can take several months to complete. If you intend to collect original data, IRB review cannot be avoided. One way of eliminating this type of time constraint is by using a "Public Use Dataset" described under "no review" below. Most universities have three levels of review:

- Full Review
- Expedited Review
- Exempt Review

Full-Board Review: Full Board reviews are not common for students performing social research. A full IRB review is normally required for studies involving greater than minimal risk. The committee collectively decides whether to approve, approve with stipulations, defer, or disapprove the study and communicates change requests if needed. If you are conducting your research at a particular facility, a second IRB review by the organization may also be required. Full reviews are conducted on a less frequent basis and can take several months to get approved. Studies involving protected groups such as children, the disabled, and other vulnerable groups require more time to review.

Expedited Review: Studies that are minimal risk and meet one or more of the expedited review criteria may be designated for expedited review by an IRB Chair or Designee. Expedited submissions are normally reviewed and approved on a rolling basis. "Expedited" review does not mean "faster", but rather only refers to a type of review for minimal risk studies. This type of review can also take a few months to get approved.

Exempt Review: An exempt study poses minimal or less than minimal risk to subjects. These types of studies do not need to go through expedited or Full Board review, but rather can be registered as exempt. Exempt research still needs to be conducted in an ethical manner and must be qualified as exempted by the IRB committee. Exempt submissions are normally reviewed on a rolling basis and should not take more than a month to be approved.

No Review: Most research projects that consist entirely of secondary data analysis do not require IRB review. Exceptions are datasets the require IRB review as a condition of acquiring a grant, or data containing social security numbers, names, or any other identifying data. Thousands of public use datasets can be found through the Federal Government, American Psychological Association, and university data centers such as ICPSR (University of Michigan), CISER (Cornell University), National Longitudinal Surveys (Ohio State University), and Murray Center (Harvard/Radcliffe). A list of web addresses is provided on the reference page.

Chapter 4. Basic Statistical Concepts

Many thesis writers think of statistics in terms of proving causality. It is more accurate to view statistics as a mechanism to explain events and to determine if those events are random. The link between specific outcomes and the inferences that can be made based on those outcomes is often not clear. In the cartoon above, the researcher is baffled because his data suggest that there is a relationship between owning a cat and being struck by lightning. While in fact, the correlation could have been statistically significant, we all know that owning a cat does not cause one to be struck by lightning. The significant relationship measured between these two variables is likely "spurious". A spurious correlation suggests the significant result is not from any direct relation between them, but from their relationship to other (mediating) variables.

Descriptive Data

Certain statistics are generated for the purpose of "describing" your data or the general relationships between variables. Descriptive statistics are widely used for presenting large amounts of data so they can be understood with minimal effort. A good example of descriptive statistics is the US Census, which provides quantified data on important household characteristics such as average household size, employment rates, ethnic and gender breakdowns, and per capita income. Descriptive statistics also include measurements of central tendency, or the center of your data set and identify if your data set is normally distributed, skewed, or has numerous outliers. Measures of central tendency include mean, median and mode.

Central Tendency

Central tendency is a measure that attempts to describe and identify the central position within that set of data and is sometimes called "a measure of central location". It also involves summary statistics including the mean (average), median and mode. The mean, median and mode are different and used differently under certain conditions.

Mean

The mean (or average) is the most popular and well known measure of central tendency. It can be used with both discrete and continuous data, although its use is most often with continuous data. The mean is equal to the sum of all the values in the data set divided by the number of values in the data set. The sample mean is usually denoted as:

$$\bar{x} = \frac{(x_1 + x_2 + \cdots + x_n)}{n}$$

It is important that the sample mean includes every value in your data set as part of the calculation. You simply add all of the values and divide the sum by the number of observations in your sample. So, if we look at the example below:

15	9	8	21	13	14	16	10	11	13

You get a total of 130 which you divide by 10 observations for a mean of 13.

Median

The median is the middle score for a set of data that has been arranged in order of magnitude. To calculate the median, suppose we have 10 scores. You simply take the middle score or two scores (in the case of an even number of observations) and average the result.

15	9	8	21	13	14	16	10	11	13

Rearrange that data in order of magnitude (smallest first):

8	9	10	11	**13**	**13**	14	15	16	21

In this data set with 10 observations you would take the average of the two middle (5th and 6th) scores. The middle scores are 13 and 13, for an average of 13. Note half of the observed scores are lower than the 13 and half of the observed scores are above.

Mode

The mode represents the score which most frequently shows up in our data set. Here "13" is the most frequently recorded score. The number is recorded twice, while the other numbers are only recorded once.

In data that are normally distributed, the mean, median and mode are equal and together represent the most typical value in the data set. In this example, we see that the mean of 13, median of 13 and mode of 13, are all equal. Therefore we can conclude that **the central tendency is at "13"** and that the data set is **normally distributed.**

Skew

Most data sets are not distributed to be perfectly normal with exactly aligned means, medians and modes. When the three measurements are not perfectly aligned, it suggests that the data is crooked or "skewed". The statistical term "skew" is used to describe unequal measurements of central tendency. When a dataset is highly skewed, you lose the ability to identify the best central location for the data.

The mean is compared to the median and mode in order to measure the degree of skew. Software programs like SPSS measure skew coefficients. Skew coefficient values below -1 and above 1 generally suggest a high degree of skew. An easy way of identifying if data is skewed is by simply calculating the mean, median and mode. The rule of thumb is:

NORMAL DISTRIBUTION
Mode = Median
Median = Mean

NEGATIVE SKEW
Mode > Median
Median > Mean

POSITIVE SKEW
Mode < Median
Median < Mean

Software such as SPSS and Excel can calculate a skew coefficient. The closer the skew coefficient is to 0, the more normally distributed the sample. Data with a skew coefficient greater than +1.0 or lower than -1.0 are generally considered asymmetrical and not normally distributed.

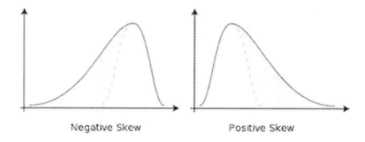

Negative Skew   Positive Skew

Figure 4.1. Negative and Positive Skew

Consider the two distributions in the figures above. Within each graph, the bars on the right side of the distribution taper differently than the bars on the left side. These tapering sides are called *tails*, and they provide a visual means for determining which of the two kinds of skew a distribution has:

1. Negative skew: The left tail is longer; the data distribution is concentrated on the right. The distribution is said to be left-tailed, or skewed to the left.
2. Positive skew: The right tail is longer; the data distribution is concentrated on the left. The distribution is said to be right-tailed or skewed to the right.

Standard Deviation

The standard deviation is a measure of the spread of scores within a set of data from a population or study sample. A standard deviation can be thought of as a "step away" from the average or mean value. One standard deviation below or above the mean captures 68% of possible observations in the sample. Two standard deviations above or below the mean capture about 95% of possible observations. Three standard deviations capture nearly all (99.7%) of possible observations. A normal distribution looks like a bell curve. The Intelligence Quotient (IQ) Test is a perfect example of a normal distribution with a mean value of 100 points and a standard deviation of 15 points. We can assume that scores for 95% of the population would fall between 100 +/- 15 or 85 and 115 points. Nearly all (99.7%) of the population is calculated as 100 +/- 45 and estimates a range between 55 and 145 IQ points. (See Figure 2)

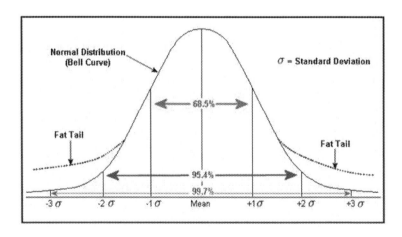

Figure 4.2. Example of a Bell Curve (Normal) Distribution

Descriptive Statistics

	N	Mean	Std. Deviation	Skewness	
	Statistic	Statistic	Statistic	Statistic	Std. Error
DASS (pre) Stress Score	60	14.03	4.407	.065	.309
Valid N (listwise)	60				

EXAMPLE: A descriptive analysis of the DASS Stress scores among this sample, revealed a mean of 14.03 and a standard deviation of 4.40 therefore, we can calculates that 95% of the observed scores are likely to be between 5.2 and 22.8 points. The skew statistic was estimated at .065, which is close to "0" and very LOW. We can assume that median, mean, and mode are close in value and the data are normally distributed.

Statistical Significance

After the null and alternative hypotheses have been identified, you need to develop a strategy for developing evidence that supports either the null or alternative hypothesis. Hypothesis testing follows a standard level of statistical significance. This is often expressed as a p-value, which is a calculated probability that your observed results were estimated by chance. You want to know whether differences are "statistically significant". Typically, you will look for a .05 or less chance that the difference in the mean value is as different as observed given the null hypothesis is true. With a p-value less than .05, you would reject the null hypothesis and accept the alternative hypothesis that there IS a significant difference. Alternately, if the chance was greater than 5%, you would fail to reject the null hypothesis and would not accept the alternative hypothesis. While the p-value of .05 is the standard level of significance used, this significance level is arbitrary. The researcher has the flexibility to place the significance cut off to a weaker (.10) or stronger (.01) value. This value must be reported clearly.

Pearson Correlation

The Pearson product-moment correlation coefficient (Pearson Correlation) is a measure of the strength of association between two variables. The Pearson product-moment correlation is often used to measure the strength of association and direction of the relationship between independent and dependent variables. However, it does not consider how the variables are classified and treats all variables equally.

The Pearson correlation coefficient is denoted by r and indicates how well the data points fit together in a model or along a line. The Pearson correlation coefficient, r, can take a range of values ranging from -1 to +1. A value of 0 indicates that there is no association between the two variables. A value greater than 0 indicates a positive association and as the value of one variable increases, so does the value of the other variable. Values less than 0 indicate a negative association. As the value of one variable increases, the value of the other variable decreases. Below are illustrations of relationships that can be found in correlations.

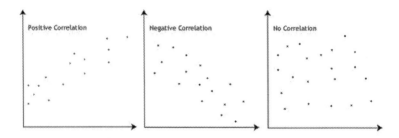

Figure 4.3 Illustration of data points and correlation directions

The strength of association based on the Pearson correlation coefficient can be determined by the coefficient r. The stronger the association of the two variables, the closer the Pearson correlation coefficient, r, will be to either +1 or -1 depending on whether the relationship is positive or negative, respectively. Achieving a value of plus or minus 1 means indicates that there is no variation in the line of best fit and the association created by the two variables is the strongest it can possibly be. By comparison, the closer the value of r is to 0, the greater the variation around the line of best fit and the weaker the association between the two variables being tested. It is important to realize that the Pearson correlation coefficient, r, does not represent the slope of the line of best fit. A Pearson correlation coefficient of (+/-) 1 suggests there is no variation between the data points and the line of best fit.

Whether or not an association is strong or "significant" depends on what you are measuring and the number of observations in your sample. However, the general guidelines for describing the strength of association by the value of r or the correlation coefficient are posted below.

	Coefficient, r	
Strength of Association	Positive	Negative
Weak	.1 to .3	-0.1 to -0.3
Moderate	.3 to .5	-0.3 to -0.5
Strong	.5 to 1.0	-0.5 to -1.0

When using a Pearson correlation coefficient to measure strength of association, your variables should be continuous, interval, or ratio scales. Examples of continuous variables include test scores, weight, and age. If you want to conduct a correlation using only ordinal or categorical data, report the Spearman's rank-order correlation instead of the Pearson correlation.

EXAMPLE: The strength in relationships between stress, gender, degree level and age group were examined using a Pearson correlation. Outcomes based on the 60 respondents suggested the relationship between stress scores and gender was not significant (r=.073, p=.582). Likewise, the relationship between stress scores and degree level *(r=-.-.038, p=.772)* and stress scores and age were not statistically significant (r=.219, p=.092). The relationships between these variables are further explored using other tests.

T-Tests

The *t*-test was introduced over a hundred years ago by a statistician named William Sealy. He devised the t-tests for Guinness brewery in Dublin, Ireland, for the purpose of cheaply monitoring the quality of beer brews and developing a trade secret. Unlike other types of tests, there are three types of *t*-test depends on what type of data you have and what you would like to measure. The three tests include:

- One-sample *t*-test
- Independent samples *t*-test
- Paired samples *t*-test

One Sample T-Test

The one-sample t-test is used to determine if the mean measurement of one sample population is significantly different from a hypothetical or known fixed mean or fixed value. The one sample t-test is appropriate to use if your dependent variable is continuous, there is no relationship between the observations, and the dependent variable is approximately normally distributed.

EXAMPLE: The average DASS stress scores for the thesis writers who responded to the study was compared to the average score reported in several publications. The average (mean) score achieved by the sample was 14.03 with a Standard Deviation of 4.4. The average stress score among adult students is about 10.5. That rate was used as the "Test Value" and compared to the mean estimated among the study sample. The outcomes estimated about a 4 point difference which was highly significant (t=6.21, p=.000). Findings suggest that the respondents in this study sample experienced a higher level of stress as measured by the DASS scale. The Ho (no difference) is therefore rejected.

One-Sample Statistics

	N	Mean	Std. Deviation	Std. Error Mean
DASS Stress Score	60	14.03	4.407	.569

One-Sample Test

	Test Value = 10.5					
					95% Confidence Interval of the Difference	
	t	df	Sig. (2-tailed)	Mean Difference	Lower	Upper
DASS Stress Score	6.210	59	.000	3.533	2.39	4.67

Two (Independent) Sample T-Tests

The independent sample t-test compares the means between two groups on the same continuous, dependent variable. For this test, the two observations from the two groups are not likely to be related and are not matched. Examples of use of the independent t-test include examining if tests scores are different by gender. In this case your independent variable would be "gender", which has two groups: "male" and "female" and dependents variable would be the test score. Another application could be testing for differences in scores before and after an intervention, assuming there is no way to pair up the results of the test scores by respondent.

To analyze your data using an independent t-test, the data should include a dependent variable that is measured on a continuous (interval or ratio) scale such as test scores, height, weight, age, etc. The independent variable should consist of two categorical, independent groups such as gender (male or female), smoker (yes or no), and so forth.

EXAMPLE: A one sample t-test was conducted to compare the average DASS stress score between degree candidates (Master's and Doctorate). Masters students received a slightly higher average score on the DASS stress scale than did Doctoral candidates, which were measured at 14.2 and 13.87 respectively. The differences however were negligible and not statistically significant (t=.291, p=.945). Therefore the Ho or null hypothesis of no difference is accepted.

Group Statistics

	Degree	N	Mean	Std. Deviation	Std. Error Mean
DASS Stress Score	Masters	30	14.20	4.536	.828
	Doctorate	30	13.87	4.345	.793

Independent Samples Test

		Levene's Test for Equality of Variances		t-test for Equality of Means						95% Confidence Interval of the Difference	
		F	Sig	t	df	Sig. (2-tailed)	Mean Difference	Std. Error Difference	Lower	Upper
DASS Stress Score	Equal variances assumed	.005	.945	.291	58	.772	.333	1.147	-1.962	2.629
	Equal variances not assumed			.291	57.892	.772	.333	1.147	-1.962	2.629

Paired (Dependent) Samples T-Test

The paired samples t-test compares the means of two related groups to detect whether there is a statistically significant difference between their mean values. To conduct this test, you need one dependent variable that is measured on a continuous, interval or ratio scales that was tested on the same subjects more than once. In the paired dependent t-test, the scores or measurements from the same subjects in each group are compared. An example of appropriate use of this test might be to compare scores before and after an intervention such as participation in a course, training or program. Care must be given to assure that the pre and post scores are properly matched for the same respondent, which may require the use of an identification code or number.

EXAMPLE: The DASS Stress sub-test scores were reported for respondents while they were writing their thesis or dissertations and tested again a month after completion. A paired t-test estimated a 1.57 point decrease. This decline in stress level was statistically significant ($t=9.16$, $p=.000$) and suggests the null hypothesis of no difference was not correct, and should be rejected. The alternative Ha suggesting a difference between the DASS score during and after the thesis writing process was significantly different.

Paired Samples Statistics

		Mean	N	Std. Deviation	Std. Error Mean
Pair 1	DASS (pre) Stress Score	14.03	60	4.407	.569
	DASS (post) Stress Score	12.52	60	3.960	.511

Paired Samples Correlations

		N	Correlation	Sig.
Pair 1	DASS (pre) Stress Score & DASS (post) Stress Score	60	.959	.000

Paired Samples Test

		Paired Differences					t	df	Sig. (2-tailed)
					95% Confidence Interval of the Difference				
		Mean	Std. Deviation	Std. Error Mean	Lower	Upper			
Pair 1	DASS (pre) Stress Score - DASS (post) Stress Score	1.517	1.282	.166	1.185	1.848	9.163	59	.000

Analysis of Variance (ANOVA)

ANOVA is similar to the t-test in that it is used to determine whether there are any significant differences in the mean values between independent (unrelated) groups. The one-way ANOVA however compares the means between **three or more groups** and determines whether any of those means are significantly different from each other. Specifically, it tests the null hypotheis (H_o) where μ = group mean and k = number of groups:

$$H_0: \mu_1 = \mu_2 = \mu_3 = \cdots = \mu_k$$

If the one-way ANOVA estimates a significant result, we accept the alternative hypothesis (H$_a$), which is that there are at least 2 group means that are significantly different from each other. It is critically important to realize that the one-way ANOVA cannot tell you which specific groups are significantly different, only that at least two groups were different. While it is assumed that when using the ANOVA the data in the dependent variable is normally distributed, ANOVA is generally a robust test against the normality assumption. Descriptive statistics such as the Mean and Standard Deviation are reported in the output along with the result from the ANOVA. When reporting the results of the one-way ANOVA, you must include the F-statistic, degrees of freedom (df), and p-value.

EXAMPLE: The average DASS Stress sub-scale was estimated for the study sample. Average scores were estimated for three age groups representing three broad age groups (30-39), (40-49) and (50 and over). While the difference in scores between the three groups was not statistically significant ($F=1.86$, $p=.164$). It was noted that students in the youngest group (30-39) scored substantially lower stress levels than did those who were in the other two age groups. For purposes of this test, we would accept the Null Hypothesis (H$_0$) of no difference.

Report

DASS Stress Score

Age Group	Mean	N	Std. Deviation
30-39	12.25	16	3.130
40-49	14.57	28	4.068
Over 50	14.88	16	5.667
Total	14.03	60	4.407

ANOVA Table

			Sum of Squares	df	Mean Square	F	Sig.
DASS Stress Score * Age Group	Between Groups	(Combined)	70.326	2	35.163	1.863	.164
	Within Groups		1075.607	57	18.870		
	Total		1145.933	59			

EXAMPLE: These findings could compel you to look at the differences in stress levels between the youngest (30-39) and oldest (50+) groups.

You could decide to run another other test (t-test) comparing these two groups (which are equal in size) for purposes of exploration. A t-test comparing only the two age groups (30-39 and over 50) indeed revealed that the 2.63 point difference between the two groups was statistically significant (t=-1.622, p=.000). From this finding, we could conclude that older students reported a higher level of stress compared to their younger counterparts.

Group Statistics

	Age Group	N	Mean	Std. Deviation	Std. Error Mean
DASS Stress Score	30-39	16	12.25	3.130	.783
	Over 50	16	14.88	5.667	1.417

Independent Samples Test

	Levene's Test for Equality of Variances		t-test for Equality of Means					95% Confidence Interval of the Difference	
	F	Sig.	t	df	Sig. (2-tailed)	Mean Difference	Std. Error Difference	Lower	Upper
DASS Stress Score Equal variances assumed	15.471	.000	-1.622	30	.115	-2.625	1.619	-5.931	.681
Equal variances not assumed			-1.622	23.374	.118	-2.625	1.619	-5.970	.720

Chi Square Test

The chi-square test is the most widely used nonparametric test used to measure if there is a relationship between two categorical variables. The chi-square test is also referred to as the one-sample goodness-of-fit test or Pearson's chi-square goodness-of-fit test can determine whether the distribution of cases (participants) in a single categorical variable (e.g. males and females) follow a known or hypothesized distribution.

When you choose to analyze your data using a chi-square test for independence, you need to make sure that two assumptions are met. First, the two variables you are testing must be **categorical**, e.g. gender (Males and Females), physical activity (sedentary, low, moderate, high), and so forth. Percentage distributions, Chi Square and p-value are reported in the output.

A chi-square goodness-of-fit test measures if the proportion of cases in each group of categorical variables is "equal" or "unequal". To use this test, variables are all categorical (dichotomous, nominal or ordinal). Examples of dichotomous variables include gender (male or female) and education level (undergraduate or postgraduate). Nominal variables can include numerous categories such as graduate schools (Business, Education, Law, Medicine, Policy, Public Health, etc.). Ordinal variables or ranking categories can reflect a likert scale value such as a level of agreement (strongly agree, agree, neither agree nor disagree, disagree, strongly disagree) or satisfaction (very satisfied, somewhat satisfied, not satisfied) and so on. To use this test, it is assumed that there is no relationship between cases or study participants and that the categorical variables are mutually exclusive.

EXAMPLE: The relationship between Stress Levels (Normal, Moderate, Severe, Very Severe) and Gender Groups (Male, Female) were estimated using a Chi Square Test. The findings found that the majority (63%) of the respondents received a stress score that was considered "very severe". A chi square test however reveled no significant differences in stress levels between genders (X^2 = 1.08, p=.58.). Therefore the Ho or null hypothesis of no difference between genders is accepted.

Stress Category * Gender Crosstabulation

			Gender Female	Gender Male	Total
Stress Category	Moderate	Count	14	4	18
		% within Gender	29.2%	33.3%	30.0%
	Severe	Count	4	0	4
		% within Gender	8.3%	0.0%	6.7%
	Very Severe	Count	30	8	38
		% within Gender	62.5%	66.7%	63.3%
Total		Count	48	12	60
		% within Gender	100.0%	100.0%	100.0%

Chi-Square Tests

	Value	df	Asymp. Sig. (2-sided)
Pearson Chi-Square	1.082[a]	2	.582
Likelihood Ratio	1.865	2	.394
Linear-by-Linear Association	.000	1	1.000
N of Valid Cases	60		

a. 3 cells (50.0%) have expected count less than 5. The minimum expected count is .80.

Dr. L.D. Molina, ScD, MPH

IRB Review

An institutional review board (IRB) is formally designated to approve and monitor research involving humans. The IRB is responsible for conducting some form of risk benefit analysis to determine whether or not research should be done. The IRB review process is conducted to assure that appropriate steps are taken to protect the rights and welfare of study participants and to protect human subjects from physical or psychological harm. IRB's are commonly used for studies in the health, social and behavioral sciences.

IRB's were initially developed in direct response to research abuses in the 20th century such as experiments performed by Nazi physicians during World War II, and the Tuskegee Syphilis Study, conducted between 1932 and 1972 by the U.S. Public Health Service. The result of many abuses both in the United States and internationally was the National Research Act of 1974 and the development of the Belmont Report. Both outline the primary ethical principles in human subjects review including "respect for persons", "beneficence", and "justice."

An IRB may only approve research for which there is a *bona fide* informed consent process for participants and for which the risks to subjects are balanced by potential benefits to society. In the United States, IRBs are governed by Title 45 Code of Federal Regulations Part 46.[2] All degree candidates performing research involving human subjects are required to go through an IRB review. Students can complete an online Human Subjects training free of charge by the National Institutes of Health, Office of Extramural Research entitled "Protecting Human Research Participants". Visit https://phrp.nihtraining.com to register and complete the free online training. Note that although NIH offers a comprehensive introduction to this topic, most universities have preferred methods and resources for training degree candidates in research ethics.

The IRB review process can take several months to complete. If your research involves collection of original data, IRB review cannot be avoided. One way of avoiding the time involved with an IRB review is by using a

"Public Use Dataset". Most universities have three levels of review and are described as:

- Full Review
- Expedited Review
- Exempt Review

Full-Board Review: Full Board reviews are not common for students performing social research. A full IRB review is normally required for studies involving greater than minimal risk. The committee discusses the study and collectively decides whether to approve, approve with stipulations, defer, or disapprove the study and communicates change requests if needed. If you are conducting your research at a particular facility, a second IRB review by the organization may also be required. Full reviews are conducted on a less frequent basis and can take several months to get approved. Note that studies involving a protected group such as children or the disabled will require more time and assurances to get approved.

Expedited Review: Studies that are minimal risk and meet one or more of the expedited review criteria may be designated for expedited review by an IRB Chair or Designee. Expedited submissions are normally reviewed and approved on a rolling basis. "Expedited" review does not mean "faster", but rather only refers to a type of review for minimal risk studies. This type of review can also take a few months to get approved.

Exempt Review: An exempt study poses minimal or less than minimal risk to subjects. These types of studies do not need to go through expedited or Full Board review, but rather can be registered as exempt. Exempt research still needs to be conducted in an ethical manner and must be qualified as exempted by the IRB committee. Exempt submissions are normally reviewed on a rolling basis and should not take more than a month to be approved.

No Review: Most research projects consisting entirely of secondary data do not require IRB reviews. The exceptions to this rule include restricted data sets or data sets funded by the National Institutes of Health and other agencies requiring an IRB review as a condition of acquiring a grant. Data sets that contain social security numbers, names, or any other identifying data may also require IRB review. Thousands of public use datasets are available for analyses through the Federal Government, American Psychological Association, and university data centers such as ICPSR (University of Michigan), CISER (Cornell University), National Longitudinal Surveys (Ohio State University), and Murray Center (Harvard/Radcliffe). A list of web addresses for these data depositories and archives is provided on the resource page.

**"In an increasingly complex world, sometimes
old questions require new answers."**

Chapter 5. Presenting Study Outcomes

Visual Presentation

Data can be presented in text, table, or chart form. Limit presented data to information and/or images that help to support any arguments and clarify points being made.

Reporting Quantitative Results

- General Practices in Reporting Quantitative Data
- Presenting Data in Charts and Graphs
  - Pie Charts
  - Bar Graphs
  - Line Graphs

Data Tables

- Tables are usually used for purposes of referencing.
- Extensive tables should be placed in appendices at the end of a report.
- Tables are typically better than graphs for structured numeric information.
- Graphs are better to illustrate trends, comparisons and relationships.
- Whole numbers under ten should be written as words, over 10 as digits.
- Be consistent with reporting decimal places. One decimal place is sufficient.
- Tables/graphs should allow the reader to understand outcomes without text.
- The title should also be informative and clearly labeled.
- Text should list key points in a table or figure only if needed.
- Statistics beyond means and frequencies should follow APA guidelines.

Charts and Graphs

Charts and graphs are often used by students to demonstrate trends in data and make comparisons between different groups or categories. There are several types of graphs choices for most efficiently and effectively presenting different types of findings.

Pie Charts

- Pie charts have limited utility and show parts of a whole equaling 100%.
- Pie charts emphasize general findings, not small differences.
- Pie charts should be used to represent categorical data with few values.
- Using 3-D graphs make pie charts can easier to see relative sizes of slices.

- Color or patterns (for black and white) facilitate comparison between slices
- Include labels or a legend next to the pie slices to which they correspond.
- Include value labels (percentages) represented by a given slice.

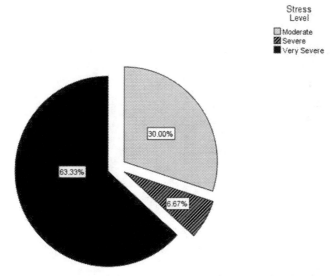

Graph 1. Distribution of (DASS) Stress Levels among Graduate Student Sample (N=60)

Bar Graphs

- Bar graphs are used for direct comparisons of data (e.g. by age group).
- Bar graphs (histograms) can be used to show normality and skew.
- Scale ranges should be standardized and not variable between graphs.
- Avoid using 3-D bar graphs so data does not look distorted.
- Stacked bar graphs are not preferred as comparisons are difficult to show.
- It is preferable to create bar graphs that group values together, side by side.

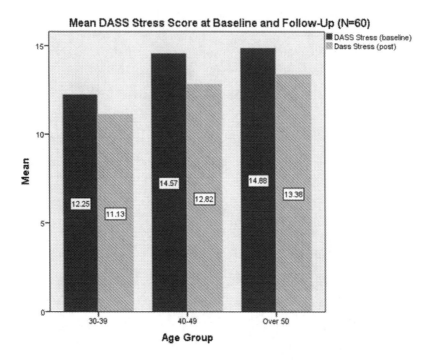

Mean DASS Stress Score at Baseline and Follow-Up (N=60)

Interval (Error Bars)

This type of graph is an excellent choice for illustrating comparisons between outcomes of continuous data by category. This type of graph:

- Provides more information than the traditional Bar Graph.
- In addition to mean (average) values, it plots the 95% confidence interval or two standard deviations (spread) below and above the mean for each category.

This type of graph is more sophisticated than the standard bar graph and demonstrates a higher aptitude for understanding your data.

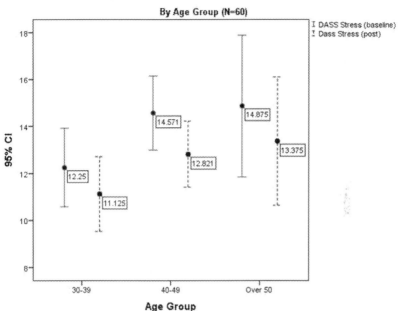

DASS Stress Scores (Mean and 95% CI) at Baseline and Follow-Up
By Age Group (N=60)

Line Graphs

Line graphs display time series data or measurements of change across time.

- Line graphs are effective for emphasizing differences over periods of time.
- The x-axis (horizontal) typically reflects time (day, week, year, etc.).
- The y-axis (vertical) illustrates frequencies or mean values being measured.
- The number of lines (categories) should be limited to avoid confusion.

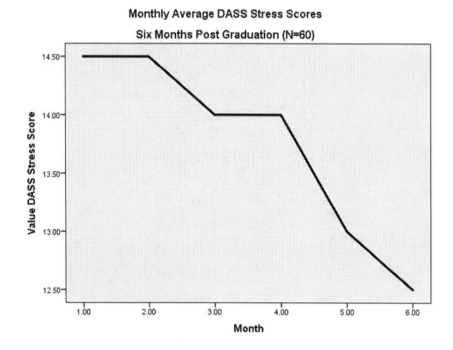

Presenting Data in Tables

- Tables are the most effective way to present data for reference purposes.
- A table should always be given a meaningful, self-explanatory title.
- The number of digits and decimal places presented should be consistent.
- It is usually better to convert counts into percentages to standardize results.
- Always include information in a table about the size of the sample.
- A table should be constructed to be easy for readers to understand.
- If possible, report outcomes in order of frequency (highest to lowest).
- Familiarize yourself with APA style when reporting scientific data.

Table 5.1.

DASS Stress Score, Gender, Degree and Age: Pearson's Correlation (N=60)

	1	2	3	4
1. DASS Stress Score	1	.072	-.038	.219
2. Gender		1	-.500**	.228
3. Degree			1	.000
4. Age Group				1

** $p \leq .01$

Table 5.2.

DASS Stress Score by Demographics: Analysis of Variance (N=60)

Demographic	n	df	M	(SD)	F	p
Gender						
Female	48	1	13.88	(4.3)	.306	.582
Male	12	1	14.67	(4.90)		
Degree						
Masters	30	1	14.20	(4.54)	.084	.772
Doctorate	30	1	13.87	(4.34)		
Age Group						
30-39	16	2	12.25	(3.13)	1.86	.164
40-49	28	2	14.57	(4.07)		
Over 50	16	2	14.88	(5.67)		

* $p \leq .05$
** $p \leq .01$

"He said our team is suffering from 'paralysis by analysis'.
Nobody knows what that means, but if it rhymes
it must be very profound!"

Chapter 6. The Final Stretch

Limitations and Delimitations

Researchers often get to the final part of their thesis without thinking about how their research approach may possibly have affected the outcomes of a study. You should think about how situations and circumstances known as limitations and delimitations may have affected or restricted the methods used and analysis of your research data. These situations should also be listed in the conclusion chapter.

Limitations are conditions or influences that the researcher cannot control. Limitations can restrict both the methodology and conclusions of your research findings. In qualitative research, findings usually cannot be generalized to the larger population. Limitations can be found in:

- The nature of self-reporting
- The instruments you utilized

- The sample
- Time constraints
- Ability to generalize findings to the population of interest

Delimitations are parameters or choices made by the researcher that can effect population or sample selection, treatment, setting, and instrumentation. Your delimitations should list and explain only the items that a reader might reasonably expect you to do within the framework of your research project including:

- Literature for review
- A particular population or study sample
- A methodological procedure

The stress sub-scale measures the degree to which the respondent feels:

- over-aroused, tense
- unable to relax
- touchy, easily upset
- irritable
- easily startled
- nervous, jumpy, fidgety
- intolerant of interruption or delay

There were several limitations and delimitations in the study used to guide the reader through this book. Among the limitations include (1) DASS Scores were all self- reported and subject to interpretation by the respondent. (2) DASS is not a diagnostic tool, but is only useful for describing the presence of a certain disturbance. (3) The sample was not random. Therefore, the findings may not be generalized.

Delimitations include (1) Using a sample of students who sought assistance with their thesis. (2) Including only "non-traditional" students who were employed, cared for a family, and/or were over 30 years of age. This could have created a biased sample of respondents who were having more difficulty and challenges with completing their thesis compared to traditional students, or those who did not need assistance with a thesis.

Discussion

You've conducted your research, analyzed your findings and written up your results. Getting this far has been exhausting, and you have little steam left to keep writing. Unfortunately, the last two chapters which consist of the discussion and conclusion sections are probably the most difficult part of the thesis to write. In your discussion, you are expected to weave together the various threads of your research. It is NOT recommended that you rush through these last two chapters. Rather, try to take a fresh look at your work in its entire and larger context. Use the discussion section as an opportunity to tell an annotated version of the story. What is your thesis about? And how will the findings affect change if any?

Conclusion

The conclusion is an important part of the thesis document. A good conclusion provides an overall picture of what the thesis is about. The conclusion should also provide a clear impression that the purpose of the thesis has been achieved. This chapter is where you share the conclusions you have reached from your research. Conclusions should stress the importance of the research and provide the reader with a sense of completeness, leaving a final impression on the reader. The conclusion is the chapter in which to (1) explore the implications of your topic or argument, (2) tie together and integrate the various issues raised in the discussion section, (3) provide answers to the thesis research question(s), (4) identify the implications of the study, (5) address the limitations and delimitations of the study, and (6) recommend direction and areas for future research.

The Abstract

Abstracts are usually the very last part of the thesis written. A concise abstract is essential. The research motivation, problem statement, approach, results, and conclusions must be included in the abstract. Abstracts can influence your reviewer to read the rest of your thesis. Similar to an "executive summary", the abstract is sometimes the *only* piece of the thesis read by committee members the people empowered to pass your thesis. The abstract should avoid vague language such as "might", "could", "may", and "seem". Placing "keywords" reduced on-line abstract text searching and assign your paper to an appropriate review category. Finally, the abstract is normally 250 words or less. Below are the essential components of an abstract.[27]

Motivation: *Why do we care* about the problem and the results? This section should include the importance of your work, the difficulty of the area, and the impact your outcomes might have.

Problem statement: What *problem* are you trying to solve? Readers should have a fundamental understanding of why the problem is important.

Approach: How did you go about analyzing or solving the problem? What important *variables* did you control, ignore, or measure?

Results: What are the results? Try to be specific and report findings, statistics or numbers that can be easily understood.

Conclusions: What are the social or practice implications of your findings? Can your results be generalized to the population from which your sample was selected?

EXAMPLE:

ABSTRACT

Students may be particularly vulnerable to stress and depression. Recently, the University of California, Berkeley reported that 47% of doctoral students and 37% of master's students met the diagnostic criteria for depression. Other universities such as the University of Michigan report that one in four of their graduate students are prescribed medication or receive counseling for depression or anxiety. This study measured stress levels for a sample of thesis writers between 2013 and 2014. A one sample T-test found that the study sample achieved an average stress score that

---

[27]   Philip Koopman (1997), <u>How to Write an Abstract</u>, Carnegie Mellon University.

was nearly 3.5 points higher than the adult population and was highly significant (t=6.2, p=.00). It was also noted that stress scores decreased from 14.0 while writing the thesis to 12.5 after completing the thesis. The 1.5 point decline was also highly significant (t=9.163, p=.00). Stress by degree revealed no difference between masters and doctoral candidates, however, stress appeared more pronounced for students over 40 years of age. These findings carry implications for addressing wellness among graduate thesis writers as well as maintaining graduate degree completion rates.

Keywords: Thesis, Stress, DASS, Age, Gender, Degree

**"Fear of public speaking is quite common.
If dressing up as Speaker Man makes you
feel more confident, then so be it."**

Chapter 7. Defense Do's Don'ts

Although each thesis has its' own uniqueness, there are some standard rules of conduct that you need to adhere to. Committees are generally consistent with what they are looking for in a candidates' defense. Below is a list of things to consider:

- Begin your presentation with a cogent summary of the study's key findings. Talk about the facts and engage in productive speculation.
- Discuss what your findings mean and how they fit in with previously published work. If your results differ from earlier research, explain why.
- Discuss how your findings might apply to your (work/professional) setting.
- Discuss the social of political implications. This is probably the most important part of a defense, but it is often overlooked.

- Limit your discussion only to the most important points.
- Emphasize the positive, but DO NOT exaggerate.
- Unless your study was a randomized experiment, avoid language that implies **causality.** Your study can only make relational conclusions, so replace words that imply causation with terms such as correlated, associated, or related.
- Emphasize interesting findings without making exaggerations or leaps.
- While it is appropriate to suggest follow-up studies, do not dwell on the future at the expense of what you have currently presented.
- You want your committee to remember you and your work. To leave your mark, show originality and creative applications for producing social change.
- Your audience will appreciate if your written document and presentation are clear and concise.

Neutrality

As a researcher, you should enter your study with a strong sense of neutrality. Neutrality is a term used to demonstrate that a research study provides an objective and unbiased view of the object under study. Procedures are developed to ensure data are valid and reliable and imply that the results are trustworthy and important. Neutrality implies that an inquiry is free of bias and is separated from the researcher's perspectives, background, position, or conditioning circumstances. A neutral researcher is implied to be trustworthy and legitimate. Legitimacy and trustworthiness are important values in all aspects of research. It is typically more difficult to achieve complete neutrality in qualitative studies.[28]

When conducting any type of study, it is critical to maintain a neutral perspective and to approach the design, collection, analysis and reporting from an unbiased perspective. This means setting aside personal perspectives to allow the findings to be interpreted and applied within ethical standards.

---

[28] Diebe, A. E., Neutrality in Qualitative Research From: M. Given (2008), Encyclopedia of Qualitative Research Methods, Sage Publications.

GLASBERGEN

**"You're getting pretty good
at this stress management thing."**

Conclusion

In this guidebook I've talked about the common experience of high stress during the thesis writing process. Data on stress collected from a sample of students with whom I have worked were used to guide you through basic concepts to help you understand ways to:

- Identify a research topic
- Ask research questions
- Formulate hypotheses statements
- Obtain a study sample
- Test hypotheses
- Present data outcomes

- Save some time and grief
- Remember that what we call "intelligence" is pliable and not fixed or stagnant. We all have the capacity to grow, learn, and fill in knowledge gaps.

The Internet offers a range of blogs and sites for exchanges with other thesis writers. Association for Graduate Student Support www.ASGS.org provides numerous resources and a consultant list. PhinisheD http://www. phinished.org provides friendly advice and support. Meetup www.meetup. com posts academic support meetings and provides the opportunity to create thesis support groups in your area. A number of discussion sites for degree candidates such as "Doctoral Students and Practitioners" are available through www.linkedin.com.

It is perfectly acceptable to ask for assistance and advice during your thesis journey. Several consulting sites can be identified online. But make sure they are legitimate and work within the parameters of academic integrity. Some services offer to sell a written thesis or write one for the inquirer. These services do not "uphold honesty and responsibility in scholarship" and should be avoided. This may seem to provide a temporary fix, but taking this route has the potential to destroy your career, and eventually, your life.

Thesis Therapy ™ is highly committed to providing services to support students towards the successful completion of their degree. We provide guidance with developing a sound study, statistical analysis, academic editing, and overcoming barriers such as anxiety, stress, and perfectionism. You are invited to visit www.ThesisTherapy.com for more information regarding services designed to help you complete your graduate thesis.

Knowledge Check

1. A recent study conducted by the U.C., Berkeley, found that about a third of Masters' students and half of Doctoral students reported symptoms of clinical depression.

A. True
B. False

2. About 80 percent of all PhD candidates eventually complete their degree.

A. True
B. False

3. Chronic stress can lead to wide range of health problems.

A. True
B. False

4. Knowledge and intellectual ability are fixed and cannot change. You're either born smart or you're not.

A. True
B. False

5. It's a good idea to test as many as variables as possible when conducting a quantitative analysis. In general, the more variables, the better.

A. True
B. False

6. Statistics are most commonly used to:

A. Determine if events are random.
B. Prove causality, or cause and effect.
C. Make generalized inferences about a populations based on results.

7. A concrete and specific prediction of what you expect will happen in your study is tested through the use of a _____.

A. Research Topic
B. Research Question
C. Hypothesis

8. Typically, the hypothesis that supports the researchers' prediction is the _____.

A. Alternative (Ha)
B. Null (Ho)
C. Two-Tailed Hypothesis (H)

9. A hypothesis that does NOT specify a direction is called a _____ hypothesis.

A. Null
B. One tailed
C. Two tailed

10. The main difference between an Experimental and Quasi-Experimental study is that the Quasi-Experimental study usually has ...

A. More variables to study
B. A non-randomized sample
C. More hypotheses to test

11. Random samples are also known as 'probability' samples because every member of the population of interest ...

A. Has an equal chance or probability of being selected to participate.
B. Will probably be asked to participate in the study.
C. Has a low probability or chance of being asked to be part of the study.

12. Which type of test is most appropriate for measuring if scores in DASS Stress levels were significantly different before and after the same sample of students completed their thesis?

A. One-Sample T-Test
B. Paired-Sample T-Test
C. Analysis of Variance (ANOVA)

13. Which type of study design is more likely to be used by the physical and clinical sciences?

A. Qualitative
B. Quantitative
C. Mixed Methods

14. Five students took the DASS stress test. The scores received for the five students were 12, 14, 12, 13 and 18. What is the MEAN among the sample?

A. 12.5
B. 13.8
C. 16.2

15. Five students took a DASS stress test. The scores received for the five students were recorded as 12, 14, 12, 13 and 18. What is the MEDIAN score?

A. 12
B. 13
C. 14

16. The scores received for the five students were 12, 14, 12, 13, and 18. What is the mode?

A. 12
B. 13
C. 14

17. Based on the three measures of central tendency, what would you expect to be the distribution of the data?

A. Normally distributed
B. Positively skewed
C. Negatively skewed

18. The DASS Stress scores are normally distributed. The mean stress score is 14.0 and the SD is 4.4. What range in scores will most likely be experienced by 95% of the sample studied?

A. 5.2 - 22.8
B. 10.8 - 16.5
C. 83 - 27.2

19. The Pearson correlation tables reported an $r=.219$ between age and stress. This Pearson's correlation coefficient suggests that the association between these two variables is:

A. Weak
B. Moderate
C. Strong

20. You have a population of 500 co-workers. You want to generate a sample with a 95% confidence level and up to a 10% margin of error. What is the minimal sample size need for this study?

A. 500
B. 125
C. 81

21. It is possible that the researcher may not require an IRB review if:

A. Only prisoners are studied
B. Respondents are not part of a vulnerable group
C. The project consists entirely of secondary data analysis of public data

22. You want to study veterans who have been chronically homeless. What type of sampling method are you most likely to use?

A. Snowballing
B. Quota
C. Self-Selection

23. Online services such as The Research Randomizer (www.Randomizer.org) provide a quick way to generate random numbers or assign participants to experimental conditions.

A. True
B. False

24. How do you define a significant result that is not from any direct relationship between two variables, but from their relationship to other (mediating) variables?

A. Co-linearity
B. Spearman's correlation
C. Spurious correlation

25. Which of the following p-values is statistically significant?

A. 98
B. 36
C. 02

26. Which graph is optimal for displaying measurements of change across time?

A. Line graph
B. Pie Chart
C. Bar Graphs with a 95% Interval

27. Scientific Data with specific measurement outcomes (e.g. P-value, T-statistic, F-statistics, etc.) is best reported not in graphs, but in data tables.

A. True
B. False

28. What section of your thesis is likely to get the closest review from committee members and other readers?

A. Introduction
B. Abstract
C. Conclusion

29. What is probably the most important, but often overlooked aspect of a thesis or dissertation defense?

A. How your results are consistent or different from earlier published work.
B. The social implications of your findings.
C. How your quasi-experimental study proves causality.

30. What is the worst thing you can do in your discussion, conclusion, or defense?

A. Fail to explain how the findings apply to your professional/personal work.
B. Limit your discussion only to the most important points.
C. Exaggerate the outcomes or the potential impact of your findings.

Answer Key

1. A   2. B   3. A   4. B   5. B   6. A   7. C   8. A   9. C   10. B
11. A   12. B   13. B   14. B   15. A   16. A   17. B   18. A   19. A   20. C
21. C   22. A   23. A   24. C   25. C   26. A   27. A   28. B   29. B   30. C

Key Terms

ANOVA (Analysis of Variance): A statistical method used to compare if mean values between two or more samples are significantly different.

Bias: The tendency of a measurement process to over- or under-estimate the value of a population parameter.

Case Study: A qualitative method which involves intensive exploration of one subject, such as a person or other unit.

Categorical Variable: Values that fall into a distinct set of categories and do not overlap such a gender (male or female).

Centrality (Measures): Measures of Centrality include mean, median and mode and designed to represent the average or middle in a distribution of data.

Confidence Intervals: The upper and lower boundaries within 95% confidence limits.

Continuous Variable: Data with a wide range of possible responses, based on a continuum such as height, weight, age, temperature, IQ, test scores, etc.

Correlation: a statistical measure that indicates the extent to which variables increase or decrease together in the same direction. Correlation does not imply causation because unknown factors can influence the relationship between the variables.

Cronbach's Alpha: A measure of internal consistency, that is, how closely related a set of items are as a group. It is considered to be a measure of scale reliability.

Cross Tabulations: Two or more variables of data are "crossed" and compared. Results can be reported as frequencies or percentages.

Data: Information collected from an experiment, survey, historical record, etc.

Delimitations: Parameters or choices made by the researcher that can effect population or sample selection, treatment, setting, and instrumentation.

Dependent Variable: The outcome caused or predicted by the independent variable.

Descriptive Statistics: Numbers used to summarize and describe data.

Dispersion: How close data cluster around the mean or measures of central tendency.

Histogram: A bar graph representing a frequency distribution and often used to illustrate normality and skew.

Hypothesis Testing: The formal procedure used to accept or reject statistical hypotheses. Hypotheses are assumptions about population parameters which may or may not be true.

Independent Measure: Different participants are used in each condition of the independent variable. Independent measures are randomly assigned and involve the use of two separate participant groups.

Independent Samples: Two or more samples selected from the same population, or different populations that have no effect on one another. An example is gender (male, female) and exposure to an intervention (treatment, non-treatment/control).

Independent Variable: Explains, causes, or predicts effects on the dependent variable.

Inferential Statistics: Outcomes based on the sample statistics are used to infer characteristics to the population represented by the sample.

Limitations: Conditions that the researcher cannot control. Common limitations include (1) inability to generalize findings to the larger population, (2) self-reporting, (3) instruments utilized, (4) sample studied, and (5) time constraints.

Matched Pairs: Two samples paired or matched by the researcher. Examples include identical twins or repeated measures for same respondent pre and post exposure.

Methodological: A process used to develop the validity and reliability of instruments to measure constructs used as variables in research.

Minimum value: The smallest observation in a set of data.

Maximum value: The largest observation in a set of data.

Mean: The arithmetic average for a group of data.

Median: The middle value in a group of data ranked in order of magnitude and where half of the values fall below and half above that middle value.

Mode: The most common value (frequency) in any distribution.

Neutrality: An objective and unbiased view of the object under study.

Normal Distribution: A bell-shaped curve or distribution which includes the mean (average) value and standard deviations.

Observation: Scientific method requires observations of nature to formulate and test hypotheses. Reproducibility requires observations by different observers be comparable. Qualitative observations can be assigned numerical values and recorded.

Ordinal Variable: Categorical data that can be ranked or ordered. Responses may have an obvious order, but the degree or value between responses may not be equal.

Outlier: An extreme value in a frequency distribution which can have a disproportionate influence on the mean. Outliers are typically 2 or more SD's away from the mean.

Parameter: A measure used to summarize characteristics of a population based on all items in the population (such as a population mean).

Population: Total set of items, demographic, or group (e.g. youth, town residents, etc.)

Probability: The likelihood that a given event will occur. Probability is quantified as a number between 0 and 1, where 0 indicates impossibility and 1 indicates certainty.

Random: In research design, random assignment is a procedure that gives each subject an equal chance of being selected to participate in an experimental or control group.

Range: A measure of dispersion calculated by subtracting the smallest value in a distribution from the largest value.

Relative Risk (RR): A comparison of the risk of a particular event for different groups of people. Relative risk is usually used to estimate exposure to something that could affect health such as a particular drug, treatment, or environmental exposure.

Reliability: Reliable assessment tools produce dependable, repeatable, and consistent information about people being studied. The reliability of a test is indicated by the *reliability coefficient,* is denoted by the letter "r," and is expressed as a number ranging between 0 and 1.00. $r = 0$ indicates no reliability, and $r = 1.00$ indicates perfect reliability. Generally, reliability of $r = .70$ is considered adequate, although r of .80 or greater is preferred.

Repeated Measures: The same participants take part in one or more conditions and tested at baseline and again at follow-up(s) or for a period of time (longitudinal). Biases include enhanced performance (practice effect), or worse performance (fatigue effect).

Sample: A subset of the population usually selected randomly. Measures that summarize a sample are called sample statistics.

Single Sample Statistic: Interested us in describing only one population. Comparing different sub-populations within the sample is not of interest.

Skew: Data distribution in which most values fall left or right of the mean.

Spread: How far observed values are from the mean. Measures of spread include range, quartile, inter-quartile, variance, and standard deviation.

Spurious Correlation: A correlation or association between variables that does not result from any direct relation between them, but from their relation to other variables.

Standard Deviation: A step away from the mean and measure of dispersion.

Statistical Test: A mechanism for making a quantitative decision about a process. The intent is to determine whether there is enough evidence to "reject" the null hypothesis.

Stratified: A method of sampling from a population. When sub-populations within an overall population vary, it is advantageous to sample each subpopulation (stratum) independently.

Target Population: An entire group of individuals or objects for which researchers are interested in generalizing the conclusions.

T-Test: A statistical examination to determine whether the two sample population means are different.

Thesis or Dissertation: A research or data driven document written as part of a qualification for an academic degree. "Thesis" typically reflects candidacy to a bachelor's or master's degree. "Dissertation" typically reflects candidacy to a doctorate. "Graduate thesis" reflects either.

Type I Error: Equivalent to false positives. The change or difference is falsely measured to be significant.

Type II Error: Equivalent to false negatives. The change or difference is falsely measured as NOT significant.

Variance: The squared value of the standard deviation.

For Further Reading

Psychology
Author: Carol
Title: Mindset: The New Psychology of Success
Paperback: 288 pages
Publisher: Ballantine Books; Reprint edition (December 26, 2007)
ISBN-10: 0345472322
ISBN-13: 978-0345472328

Research Design
Author: John W. Creswell
Title: Research Design: Qualitative, Quantitative, and Mixed Methods Approaches
Paperback: 273 pages
Publisher: SAGE Publications, Inc.; 4th edition (March 14, 2013)
ISBN-10: 1452226105
ISBN-13: 978-1452226101

SPSS/Statistics
Author: Andy Field
Title: Discovering Statistics using IBM SPSS Statistics
Paperback: 952 pages
Publisher: SAGE Publications Ltd; 4th edition (January 24, 2013)
ISBN-10: 1446249182
ISBN-13: 978-1446249185

Writing/Formatting
Author: American Psychological Association
Title: Publication Manual of the American Psychological Association
Paperback: 272 pages

Publisher: American Psychological Association (APA); 6th edition (July 15, 2009)
ISBN-10: 1433805618
ISBN-13: 978-1433805615

Author: Kate L. Turabian (Author), Wayne C. Booth, Gregory G. Colomb (Editors)
Title: A Manual for Writers of Research Papers, Theses, and Dissertations, 8th Edition
Paperback: 464 pages
Publisher: University Of Chicago Press; 8th edition (March 28, 2013)
ISBN-10: 0226816389
ISBN-13: 978-0226816388

Free Online Resources

Create Online Surveys
https://www.surveymonkey.com
https://kwiksurveys.com
http://www.zoomerang.com

Human Subjects/Ethics/Institutional Review Board
https://phrp.nihtraining.com

Public Data Sets
American Psychological Association (APA) http://www.apa.org/research/responsible/data-links.aspx
ICPSR (University of Michigan) http://www.icpsr.umich.edu
CISER (Cornell University) https://www.ciser.cornell.edu
Federal Government http://www.data.gov/
National Longitudinal Surveys (Ohio State) https://www.chrr.ohio-state.edu
Murray Center (Harvard/Radcliffe) http://www.murray.harvard.edu

Statistics Calculator
http://www.socscistatistics.com/tests/
http://www.mathportal.org/calculators/statistics-calculator
http://www.openepi.com

Sample Randomizer
https://www.randomizer.org

Sample Size Calculator
http://www.surveysystem.com/sscalc.htm
http://www.raosoft.com/samplesize.html

Dr. L.D. Molina, ScD, MPH

Statistics Review

https://ihatestatistics.com
http://www.statisticshelp.org
http://www.mathportal.org/calculators/statistics-calculator
http://www.psychstat.missouristate.edu

References

Andrews, M., Doctoral Degrees Gain Steam in Healthcare Industry, U.S. News, World Report, March 20, 2012.

Agency for Clinical Innovation, Australia (2015). From: http://www.aci.health.nsw.gov.au/__data/assets/pdf_file/0019/212905/DASS_21_with_scoring_BB.pdf.

Andrews, M. Doctoral Degrees Gain Steam in Healthcare Industry, U.S. News, World Report, March 20, 2012.

Azar, B., Discussing your findings. Your dissertation's discussion should tell a story, say experts. What do your data say? American Psychological Association, www.apa.org/gradpsych/2006/01/findings.aspx. Retrieved on July 2, 2015.

Bear, J. and Ezzell, A., Does Your Doctor Have a Fake Degree? The Billion-Dollar Industry That Has Sold over a Million Fake Diplomas retrieved June 18, 2013 from: http://www.alternet.org/story/155864.

Council of Graduate Schools launched the PhD Completion Project htp://www.phdcompletion.org/information/executive_summary_demographics_book_ii.pdf.

Dweck, C., (2007) Mindset: The New Psychology of Success, Random House Pub.

Fruscione, J. When a college contracts 'adjunctivitis,' it's the students who lose, PBS News Hour, WGBH, July 25, 2014

Haynie, D. Experts Debate Graduation Rates for Online Students. U.S. News World Report, Jan. 30, 2015.

Ivey, J.B., DSN, CRNP, Health Policy and the DNP Student. Topics in Advanced Practice Nursing eJournal. 2008; 8 (4).

Leung R., Diplomas for Sale: Reports on Online Diploma Mills, CBS News, November 8, 2004.

Lindley, J. & Machin, S. The boom in postgraduate education and its' impact on wage inequality. Center for Economic Performance, London School of Economics, Economics Report, November 20, 2013.

McLeod, S. A. (2007). *Experimental Design - Simply Psychology.* Retrieved from http://www.simplypsychology.org/experimental-designs.html.

Palok, A., Potter, A. Griebel, P. Modern approaches to understanding stress and disease susceptibility: A review with special emphasis on respiratory disease, International Journal of General Medicine 2009:2 19–32.

Radyuhin, Vladimir, Fake doctorates: Russia to crack down on academic fraud. The Hindu, Moscow Russia, February 21, 2013.

Segran, E. The Adjunct Revolt: How Poor Professors Are Fighting Back, The Atlantic, April 28, 2014.

Seward, Z. MIT Admissions Dean Resigns after Fake Degrees Come to Light. Diplomas from three schools were fabricated, school officials say, *The Crimson,* Harvard University, April 26, 2007.

Sheehy, K. (2013) Online Course Enrollment Climbs for 10th Straight Year. U.S. News. From: http://www.usnews.com/education /online-education/articles/2013/01/08/online-course-enrollment -climbs-for-10th-straight-year.

Staff writers, (2015) UC Berkeley graduate students exhibit high rates of depression, survey says. The Daily Californian, University of California, Berkeley. Wednesday, April 22, 2015.

Staff writers, (2015) Depression common on college campuses; graduate students more at risk, The Conversation, May 9, 2015. http://www.psypost.

org/2015/05/depression-common-on-college-campuses-graduate-students-more-at-risk-34158.

Trochim, W. (2006) Research Methods Knowledge Base. Retrieved From: http://www.socialresearchmethods.net/kb/desexper.php.

Urbaniak, G. C., & Plous, S. (2013). Research Randomizer (Version 4.0). From http://www.randomizer.org.

U.S. Census, Computer and Internet Use in the United States: 2013 By Thom File and Camille Ryan, Issued November 2014. From: http://www.census.gov/history/pdf/2013computeruse.pdf

U.S. Department of Education, IES, National Center for Education Statistics (20014). https://nces.ed.gov/programs/digest/d13/tables/dt13_318.20.asp.

U.S. News staff, Enrollment Climbs for 10th Straight Year. From: http://www.usnews.com/education/online-education/articles/2013/01/08/online-course-enrollment-climbs-for-10th-straight-year. Retrieved on June 20, 2015.

Winerman, L., (2014) Ten years to a doctorate? Not anymore. Psychology programs are trying new ways to speed students' progress toward their degrees. American Psychological Association, Washington, DC.

Worster A. and Haines, T, Advanced Statistics: Understanding Medical Record Review (MRR) Studies, Academy of Emergency Medicine, Vol.11, No.2. February 2004.

Printed in the United States
By Bookmasters